Thankyou for supporting "The Recovering Farmer"

Gerry

THE RECOVERING FARMER

A Journey through the Labyrinth of Anxiety and Depression

by Gerry Friesen

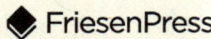
FriesenPress

One Printers Way
Altona, MB R0G 0B0
Canada

www.friesenpress.com

Copyright © 2024 by Gerry Friesen
First Edition — 2024

Photographer: Tony Friesen

This book is intended to provide information and insights based on the author's learning and experiences. It is not meant to serve as medical advice for anyone living with a mental illness. This book is simply a collection of what worked for him. Additionally, the author may not be aware of existing intellectual property rights or attributions related to specific thoughts, concepts, ideas or commonly used sayings presented in this book.

All rights reserved.

No part of this publication may be reproduced in any form, or by any means, electronic or mechanical, including photocopying, recording, or any information browsing, storage, or retrieval system, without permission in writing from FriesenPress.

ISBN
978-1-03-830613-5 (Hardcover)
978-1-03-830612-8 (Paperback)
978-1-03-830614-2 (eBook)

1. BIOGRAPHY & AUTOBIOGRAPHY, PERSONAL MEMOIRS

Distributed to the trade by The Ingram Book Company

Dedication

To Rose
My caring and supportive partner.
You never gave up on the seemingly impossible.
Look how far we've come.

Table of Contents

Foreword		vii
Introduction		1
Chapter 1	The Beginning: Naming the Beast	7
Chapter 2	Was I a Farmer? An Identity Crisis	15
Chapter 3	Relationships are Important: A Significant Other	26
Chapter 4	What Have I Done? The Reality Hits Hard	37
Chapter 5	The Hatchet Twins: Partners in Crime	46
Chapter 6	This Happened to Me: Farming with Reckless Abandon	55
Chapter 7	A Mennonite: To Be or Not to Be	64
Chapter 8	When Columbus Sailed the Ocean Blue: Discovering the Giant Within	75
Chapter 9	Can We All Just Get Along? Turning Judgement to Curiosity	83
Chapter 10	Talking About it Helps: A Passion for Mental Wellness in Agriculture	97
Chapter 11	Who Am I? A Piece of the Puzzle, But Where Does It Fit?	108
Chapter 12	The Journey: Weathering the Storm	115
Chapter 13	My Addiction: Coming Out of the Closet	128

Chapter 14	Afraid of Living: But I Don't Want to Die	139
Chapter 15	Don't Suffer in Silence: Building a Bridge	146
Chapter 16	What Works for Me: Taming the Beast	157
Chapter 17	A Random Act of Kindness: The Cuddle Hormone	175
Chapter 18	Working on a Puzzle: Don't You Quit	182
Acknowledgements		189
About the Author		193

Foreword

Here's the thing. You can write about your lived experiences with depression and addiction by dropping your bucket to the bottom of your own well and pulling up the mud, silt, murk, and pain of it all.

So that story would be sensationalized to a degree, entertaining and voyeuristic, but does it help anyone else?

Instead of that type of story, in *The Recovering Farmer*, Gerry Friesen has chosen another route, another path for us to follow, through storytelling and scene setting.

One might call this journey "the high road of a low road." Friesen's book walks you through his life and how he experienced addiction and depression. Anecdotally, being a farmer, Friesen should know what came first, the cart or the horse, the chicken or the egg, the addiction or the depression. Whatever the sequence, the combination is brutal and unforgiving.

Friesen doesn't avoid the agonies of well, these dual agonies. He doesn't make this a duel of which is worse or which comes first. There is no redemptive value in spending time sorting that out. His words are spent on illuminating cause and effect and outcomes. The impacts on family, friends, himself, his work, and his life. The agonies are there from both addiction and depression.

He has an extraordinary sense of situational awareness in dealing with others. Talking about depression, and to some extent addiction, with someone who hasn't experienced these demons, is sometimes next to impossible. Friesen, however, has lived it, obviously gets it, so his storytelling can be consumed in an almost liquid manner. The chapters flow into you easily, like drinking a cold Diet Coke on a hot day.

Friesen's self-disclosure is a unique truth serum. Humble, humorous, and honest. Never a whiff of "look at me" or "woe is me." Friesen doesn't share his story for glory or gain. He just shares because he believes sharing helps him and may help others. More than anything, *The Recovering Farmer* addresses the stigma of mental illness. Friesen advocates the benefit of transparency on mental health, and more importantly, that depression and addiction are sicknesses, not weaknesses. They need to be seen in the light of day, not in darkness. The implicit advocacy inherent in his writing will bring people to this light whether they themselves are affected by depression or addiction or not.

The writing is crisp, somewhat spare in locations, but still with the colour required to paint the pictures this recovering farmer is sharing. Friesen's composition is a genuine mixture of humour, honesty, and learning. The format of the book is compelling. He leads with intriguing chapter names that grab and pull you in. Then he provides an anecdotal set-up for what is to come and finishes with a takeaway. He ties the bow on every chapter.

The Recovering Farmer can be a very quick read. Don't do that! Read a chapter and reflect.

You don't have to be farmer to harvest value from the seeds Friesen plants. This book is universally accessible, relatable, and meaningful to all those impacted by mental health issues and addiction and the people that support them.

Envision yourself as a recovering farmer, maybe on a porch on a sun-filled day, knowing that battles with addiction and depression never go away. Thinking, reflecting on it all and facing these ills for what they are, just that, ills. Understanding them as best we can, sharing them with others we trust and love. Then maybe, just maybe, we can enjoy that day on the porch.

Gerry, thanks for a good day on the porch.

Michael McMullen, Author

Introduction

I am chatting with a farm couple at their kitchen table. Emotions are running high as they describe their financial challenges to me. The stress has left them tired. It has created relational issues between the two of them and their children, who are farming with them. He pulls out a letter they have received from their lender. His voice breaks as he reads the letter to me. The lender has provided notice that they are poised to push them into receivership. As he finishes, I look at him and relate how I dealt with a similar letter from my lender. His eyes open wide and his jaw drops. And then he says in a questioning way, "You know what this is like?" That connection took the farm couple from feelings of helplessness to feelings of hope. Or perhaps not hope as much as the realization that they were not alone, there were others that had experienced what they were going through. That connection opened the door for a good discussion on how best to address their situation.

Over the years, as I have shared tidbits of my story, I often questioned how much I should share. I have always been one, much to the chagrin of my wife, who keeps stories short, to the point and lacking details. But I found that with each interview or presentation I would open up more and share more details of my journey. Many appreciated hearing about my journey, but there were those who found it curious that I had the freedom to talk about mental illness.

There were times when I too questioned my freedom to share. And then one day it occurred to me. The reason I could share openly and freely was that "talking about it" has given me freedom. Sounds strange, I know. But there is a freedom in being able to come out of isolation, to be able to talk openly about those things that are dragging me down, to be able to articulate the darkness that can so easily overwhelm.

I have had the opportunity to interact with countless people in the work I do. It began in 2000 when I became involved in farm debt mediation work. And continued and grew in 2007 when I became involved with a farm stress line. Most of the folks I talked to were experiencing significant stress. The conversations with many of them encouraged me to talk openly about my mental health challenges. It became evident early on that sharing openly created connection, helped others open up, and through that, found ways of moving forward. For them, but also for myself. I often felt like I was getting more than I was giving.

The story at the outset is but one example of innumerable conversations I have had. As I thought about that, I was also reminded of another response I had received. In 2018 I participated in an interview where I shared my story. Since first telling my story in 2010, I had made significant progress in understanding my mental illness and, by extension, had many more insights to share. After the interview aired, a listener reached out and made the following comment: "Thank you for your interview. I pulled over, cried, and for the first time in weeks felt like I wasn't drowning. You have no idea the impact you have."

Because of stories like that, I thought that writing about my own journey could be helpful to others. You see, it's a story within a story. Let me rephrase that. It's a story within a title. It covers many aspects of my life. A life that has had its fair share of twists

Introduction

and turns. A life with ups and downs. A life of discovery. A life of experience. It has been suggested that experience is what you get when you don't get what you want. That simply means I seldom got what I wanted, because I have lots of experience. Furthermore, someone told me recently that experience is something you get right after you need it. Isn't that the truth! With the experience I have today, it would be a lot easier handling many of the situations of bygone days.

But it is not that simple. I have made discoveries, particularly in the last few years, that tell me there is a lot more to my stories, more to life. But it requires a starting point. Perhaps as you read this book you will feel that I am sharing my pain. Although my pain does shape and form my story, my intent is to provide hope. I would love to be able to start my story with "once upon a time" and end it with "I lived happily ever after." But that would not be reality. It is more a story of a journey, and a journey must have a beginning, and the ending (spoiler alert) is simply me telling you that the journey continues.

As such, a journey needs to start somewhere. Although I was diagnosed with anxiety and depression in 2004, I began to understand that my journey had started much before that. As I began mapping it out, I realized quickly that my journey had started at a young age. And all I had been involved in contributed in some way, shape, or form to where I am at today.

My hope is that this will not be perceived as a blame game. We often hear of folks that blame their upbringing, the church they went to, the strict teacher in school, or a variety of other issues or events they have experienced, for the struggles they may be experiencing today. That is not my intent. But I believe it is important, at least for me, to look at and understand how life's experiences contribute, negatively or positively, to my mental wellbeing.

Confronting the past is not always easy. Over the course of my writing, the past would often come back to haunt me. I remembered some of the challenges I encountered that still leave me feeling raw. For instance, the memory of my addictions still lingers, casting a shadow on my thoughts. They were constant reminders of how life's uncertainties can bring us to our knees.

Moreover, revisiting the past allowed me to understand how many parts of my journey had negatively impacted those close to me. I could recall the strain my mental illness placed on my family, particularly my wife and kids. The despair I felt at the time infected our household, draining any semblance of joy from our lives.

And when that happened, the writing would stop. I would find myself becoming discouraged. But then through conversations with others or something I read, I would find some clarity, come to understand that the past is the past and not something to be dwelled upon. And when I suggest the past is the past, I do not diminish the impact it had on my journey. I discovered that each piece of my past helped shape and mold who I am today.

I also made another important discovery. I found that writing about my life was therapeutic. With the state of my mental health, it is easy to get lost in negativity. And when in that state of mind, it becomes even easier to view my life as a waste. But as I thought about all I had done and been involved in, I found the narrative in my brain begin to change. I realized that all my experiences, both positive and negative, were steppingstones to a brighter future. Then again, this may be a cry for help. God knows, I need help.

Many years ago—too many to remember—I had the thought that should I ever write my life story I would call it *Pigs, Politics, and Diet Coke*. I was working at the farm and must have been mulling over my life, thinking about *who* I was and *what* I was. As you will find out if you keep reading, I was a pig farmer. I can't dispute that. And even when I tried, the smell in the air gave it away. I was involved in agricultural politics and had some aspirations of moving on to provincial politics. Today I scratch my head at that one and am thankful I never followed through. When I was

Introduction

able to control my addictions, I drank copious amounts of Diet Coke. Based on supposed research of the effects of Coke on our bodies, I probably shouldn't be alive.

Then shortly after the wind down of my farm, I began calling myself The Recovering Farmer. It wasn't until a few years later that I became curious as to what that really meant. That curiosity was largely driven by a phone call I got from my sister after she heard an interview I had done on the radio where the host referred to me as that. She asked me what "recovering farmer" really meant. I did not have an answer for her but decided I needed to look into it, particularly if I wanted to keep referring to myself as that.

I suspect that I must have had the term "recovering alcoholic" in mind when I came up with the pseudonym The Recovering Farmer. In that context, the word recover means to return to a former state of well-being, prosperity, and emotional balance. In my case, the emotional balance piece has been particularly challenging, largely due to my mental health issues. I like to use the word equanimity, which simply means having mental and emotional stability, especially in difficult or challenging situations. So it's clear to me that I have not recovered, but rather, I am working at it and find myself making progress.

Over the course of the last number of years I have been the recipient of some awards. I say recipient because suggesting I won awards just doesn't sit right with me. How is living a life with anxiety, depression, and addiction award worthy? What I did do is open up and talk about my mental health or lack thereof. I learned early on that talking about it helps. We learn from each other. Receiving those awards confirmed for me that by showing vulnerability, I was making a difference.

I also often think that it isn't me that deserves any awards, because if not for some significant people around me, there would not have been any awards, and this journey would have turned out quite differently. My wife and kids deserve awards for the support they provided, the strength they have shown, and their ability to show love under difficult circumstances. That became evidently clearer as I wrote.

This book does not offer researched medical or psychological information to provide answers, as it is not a self-help guide in that sense. I often feel more comfortable in describing the problem than charting a course for it. So it's a story of one person's experiences and lessons learned. Feel free to read it at your discretion, laugh if you can, shed a tear if necessary, and approach it with an open mind. Within its pages you might well discover information that could prove helpful on your own life's journey.

Chapter 1
The Beginning: Naming the Beast

I feel out of my element. Together with a colleague, we are sitting and talking to a couple involved in hog production who are facing some significant decisions due to their financial situation. Quickly, and without warning, my heart starts palpitating, flopping around like a fish out of water. Along with that comes a shortness of breath. I feel lightheaded. Without appearing too obvious, I grab the table, convinced I will pass out. All I can think is that I am having a heart attack and am about to die.

In 2003 I was operating a family farm in western Manitoba. I was the president of Manitoba Pork Marketing, the chairman of Dynamic Pork, and an active mediator with the Manitoba Farm Mediation Board. The hog industry was in a continuous downward spiral. My farm, the folks I was assisting in farm debt mediation, the organizations I was involved in, and its members, were experiencing significant challenges.

The heart palpitations and shortness of breath puzzled me. Although they passed relatively quickly that first time, it started happening more often, to the point where in early 2004 I went to see my doctor.

After hearing my description of what was happening, he was quick to suggest that I was experiencing anxiety attacks which, if they hadn't yet, could ultimately lead to depression. I had no reason to question his judgement. And it *was* a judgement, because there really are no X-rays or blood tests that can be done to detect anxiety or depression.

I always liked that doctor. He had emigrated from South Africa to rural Manitoba. Outside of his medical practice, he also dabbled in farming. We would quickly get the medical stuff out of the way and then chat about farming. And getting the medical stuff over with normally involved a prescription.

He sent me home that day with a prescription for antidepressants. He warned me that the antidepressants would increase my symptoms before things would start getting better. Without any thought of the implications, I started on the medication. Little did I know how bad it would get. In my naivety, I just thought that life would get better.

The doctor was right. The next few weeks I ceased to function. Essentially, I spent my time on the couch, grappling with the overwhelming anxiety that engulfed my mind. The clouds of depression grew even darker than before. The moment I got out of bed in the morning, pressure built in my head, my stomach churned, and my thoughts turned bleak.

In my mind, I was convinced that should I die, my wife and kids would be better off. My life insurance would kick in and ease the financial burden for all, my family could live a better life, and I would be rid of the pain I was experiencing. The simple thought was that if I could not provide for them in life, by dying I could.

During those dark times, my wife would leave for work in the morning, never knowing what she would find when she got home. She and my brother collaborated, making sure he would check on me while she was at work. And for good reason. Although I have

Chapter 1   The Beginning: Naming the Beast

always said I did not plan on killing myself, at the time, my mind was busy thinking how I could, should I choose to.

At times it was difficult to comprehend that I still had a farm that I needed to get back to. All the stressors I experienced before the doctor appointment still hung over my head. Our financial situation was not improving, and our creditors were getting nervous. I needed to prepare financial projections for our bank to get our operating line of credit renewed. The outlook for hogs was not great, so that was going to create issues. We had to change feed companies as our credit and their patience had run out. I needed to keep our barn in production so kept buying weanlings but needed to shuffle finances in order to pay for ongoing expenses. That meant we had to ship hogs that would not be heavy enough to maximize returns, but to juggle everything, I had no choice.

There were numerous mediation files I needed to deal with. Many of my clients were in a similar situation as I was. One in particular was facing imminent bankruptcy. Just seeing that name come up on my call display sent my anxiety skyrocketing. Other clients had to get their bank credit arranged and approved just to continue operating. The phone calls never ended. On top of that, the Manitoba government had asked me to mediate between two organizations. Progress on that was slow and the pressure from government was intense for me to get an agreement in place.

The marketing organization I was president of needed to finalize pricing for the upcoming year. The negotiations were difficult as the processors also needed to change their operations to deal with negative margins. In addition to that, the production units the organization was involved in were dealing with challenges of their own. That meant countless meetings and discussions to seek solutions.

Six weeks after starting on meds I had still not been able to go to the barn. My brother had graciously agreed to take on some of my responsibilities to give me a break. But over time his work was taking him away from the farm, so most of the work fell on our hired man.

Then on a Sunday morning, my hired man phoned to tell me he needed help sorting and loading hogs. I knew we needed cash flow to meet our financial obligations. We needed to make room for more weanlings. That meant going to the barn and facing reality. I knew it would be a challenge finding enough market-ready pigs. I knew that chasing pigs would increase my anxieties.

As much as I was already experiencing anxiety, the thought of going to the barn, working with pigs, knowing the challenges I would face, exponentially increased it. I started pacing the floor. I grabbed a Bible and read a verse that assured me that God knew what I was going through and would help me. I prayed diligently—all to no avail. Ultimately, I had no choice, I had to go.

I did face reality that day, and it was just as bad as I had anticipated. It was difficult to really care. I wanted to get the job done and head back to the security of the couch. Facing reality was difficult, but I also understood that I had limited choice. I realized that all the things pushing me towards the abyss were not going away by avoiding them. I knew that as much as life was worrying, I needed to push onward, understanding that all worrying does is create something in our mind that we don't want to have happen. As much as it was difficult, I knew I needed to start moving forward, even if it was but one small step at a time.

Those six weeks away from the farm provided ample time for me to analyze my life. I thought long and hard about the decision I had made to go into farming. I wondered how my upbringing in a conservative home and church had contributed to my mental health or lack thereof. I wondered why I had jumped into the agricultural political arena. I was curious about my continuous low self-esteem. I was puzzled by a seeming inability to have meaningful relationships. Although I had quit drinking, those desires persisted, particularly because of my overwhelming anxiety. Most

Chapter 1   The Beginning: Naming the Beast

of the answers I came up with did not satisfy. There was no clarity. As much as the medication was creating a chemical balance in my brain, life was still somewhat of a mystery for me.

During those dark, anxious days of reflection, I came to understand that this was not the beginning of my mental illness. At a young age, something as benign as my dad getting stuck in the snow on a Sunday night would create intense anxiety for my bus ride the following day. My parents literally had to push me onto the school bus. I did not want to ride the bus, as I was convinced it would end in tragedy. I did not want to go to school, because I knew I would be bullied.

I thought back to my teenage years and remembered some of the anxiety I experienced at the time. Although all these years later it was not easy to identify what specifically caused the anxiety, I did recognize that often when things happened, I would be filled with fear and uncertainty.

Growing up on a farm meant that at an early age I would be sent to the field for the day. As I did not have a driver's licence, I would drive a smaller tractor to the field, start a bigger tractor, and cultivate all day. Being alone all day gave me ample time to think of a variety of things that were scary. What if I had a breakdown? What if I got hurt? God forbid, but what if I was killed?

Being part of a fundamental Mennonite home, there was the constant fear of wondering whether my heart was right with God. It always seemed that I was just not finding the peace that I was assured of if only my heart was right. That peace and the ultimate promise of heaven was so elusive. At the time, I was convinced that my anxiety was guilt. I would pray and confess but nothing took away the churning anxiety. It became difficult to sleep at night, not knowing whether I was "good."

As I came out of the teen years and began the next stage of life, I never had the confidence I needed to do the work I was tasked with. If I was sent out to do a job that included an overnight stay away from home, I would have anxiety to the point of not being able to eat. I would seriously consider ways of hurting myself at work, just so I could go home, to escape the anxiety I was feeling. I needed to be creative in coming up with some excuse when I was tasked with jobs that entailed me working alone.

I remembered periods where I fell into a depression, although I did not recognize it at the time. I just did not feel like seeing people. I did not want to talk to my brother or my wife. In essence I was a zombie, trying to make it from one day to the next. There was no joy in life.

I reflected on my coping skills, and they had not been healthy or helpful. Perhaps part of it may have been the mindset that I needed to work harder. Smoking and drinking had been part of my life. I know I was often irritable and quick to anger. I had tried hiding my mental illness from my wife and kids. I would find sanctuary in my barn, away from my family, away from my office, away from my phone, and probably trying to escape from myself. I was caught in a vicious cycle. And the more I tried to get out of that cycle, the more I seemed to be moving in the wrong direction.

Although I came to understand some of my mental illness, the 2004 diagnosis was more a start to recovery. It was difficult to acknowledge the sickness because I thought it was a weakness. The stigma got in the way of being proactive. I was avoiding naming the beast.

It would become increasingly clear that I was on a journey in a labyrinth of anxiety and depression. Labyrinths are often used as a metaphor for life's journey—not necessarily a mystery to be solved, but rather a path to finding meaning. Those paths are circular and complex, taking us through twists and turns. While one may not truly become lost within them, although it may feel that way, it can be difficult to determine where you are headed and how long the journey may be.

Chapter 1   The Beginning: Naming the Beast

It would take many years before I would find out how that describes my journey. It would take some time before I would understand the importance of those close to me walking with me. Only when I began the discovery part of my journey and was able to name the beast was I able to begin the process of getting better. But that came much later.

Takeaway

Mental illness indirectly affects all of us. We experience it personally. Or we see family, friends, or colleagues dealing with it. Interestingly enough, the onset usually occurs in adolescence or early adulthood. What is puzzling for many is the cause, which can be a combination of genetics, biological factors, and environmental factors.

Mental illness is an insidious sickness that can be difficult to diagnose and even more difficult to treat. It hits in a variety of different ways and is far from consistent from one individual to the next. It can affect us physically, emotionally, mentally, and spiritually. As that happens, our behaviours change. It's not always easy to understand what is happening till we seek help from a professional who can connect the dots for us and offer treatment options.

Regrettably, there continues to be a significant societal stigma surrounding mental illness. This attitude is not surprising when examining historical perspectives. Before the eighteenth century, mental illness was frequently attributed to evil spirits or demons. While some eventually began to perceive mental illness as a medical condition, it remained widely considered incurable. Lobotomies and electric shock treatments were attempted as interventions. It wasn't until the 1950s that medication emerged as a viable treatment option. Thanks to ongoing advancements in research and development, medication has now become a primary approach to addressing mental illness. Additionally, psychotherapy and counseling have gained traction as treatments and are often done in conjunction with medication.

Getting an accurate diagnosis, or naming the beast, is important in moving forward in the healing process. It is critical for establishing the basis of any treatment. There is no way of healing if you're not willing to name the beast. Not knowing or avoiding naming the beast leads to wasting time, leaves your life in limbo, and prevents you from moving forward. Recovery requires discovery. So in addition to naming the beast, it is important to learn and discover as much as possible about your mental health, because with understanding and awareness comes the ability to utilize a variety of tricks and tools to increase and achieve mental wellness.

Chapter 2
Was I a Farmer?
An Identity Crisis

On a cool fall evening in 2007 I made my way into a Boston Pizza. My work frequently took me to Winnipeg, and this evening, a meal with my kids offered a welcomed respite. The last year had been particularly difficult, as I was trying to wind down the farm, giving up a way of life that had defined me for so long. I was mentally and emotionally exhausted. As I walked in, I met someone I knew, a feed salesman I got to know through my involvement in the hog industry. He asked how I was doing. I told him about winding down and selling our farm. I suggested to him that I didn't think I was a farmer anymore. In response, he met my gaze and suggested, "perhaps you never were."

Later that night I thought about what that salesman had said to me. I knew he had not said what he did to disparage me. In my mind there were different ways of looking at this. Perhaps I had been a farmer but failed miserably. Maybe I had never had the ability to farm but tried anyway. Or maybe he had long recognized my strengths in other areas and felt my time spent farming was not productive. Clearly, I was experiencing an identity crisis.

There are times when I wish that someone had suggested I really wasn't a farmer before I went farming! I see so many other things that could have provided for a better life, better career, and better end result. However, as others remind me of quite often, had it not been for my life experiences as a farmer I would not be doing now what I am doing. In essence, had I not gone broke, had I not had addiction issues, and had I not slipped into a world of anxiety and depression, I could not do what I am doing. Although I now understand that better, accepting it has not been easy.

Of course, that brings about the question: Was it meant to happen? Back in January of 2012 my son and I had a discussion about whether things were meant to happen. At the time we were referring to some significantly negative things that were being experienced by people close to us. I suppose that question could also be asked when something really positive and perhaps unexpected happens, but we seldom do. We agreed that people experience positives and negatives in their lives. We enjoy the positives and accept the negatives as simply being part of the imperfect world we live in. A short week after that discussion, something happened that made me rethink that discussion.

For two years my wife and I had been contemplating a move closer to Winnipeg. Part of that challenge was that my wife had a good job in Wawanesa, and if we wanted to move it would require her to find employment near Winnipeg. Yes, I was still working, but being self-employed meant that I could carry on with my work regardless of where we lived. We had an ongoing discussion. I was of the belief that she needed to find a job before we moved, and she was of the opinion that she could find a job after our move.

Twice over the previous two years we had listed our home for six month stretches. There was little, if any, interest shown, and so we were beginning to wonder whether we would be able to sell. Then on January 16 she received a call that she had qualified for a job near Winnipeg if she wanted it. In a flash, life became somewhat

Chapter 2 Was I a Farmer? An Identity Crisis

overwhelming. We agreed that she should accept the job. She was quite confident that if it was meant to be—selling the house and buying a new house would happen smoothly. I wasn't convinced.

Not having had much luck with real estate agents, we put our house on Kijiji that night. I was convinced that my wife would be moving to Winnipeg while I stuck around Wawanesa for however long to sell our house. However, that was not to be. Within two weeks our house had sold, and we had purchased a house in La Salle, a community near Winnipeg. A month and one day from when she got the job offer, we moved.

All of that got me reconsidering my earlier opinion on whether things were meant to happen. Based on the way things fell into place, how the stars appeared to line up, I really wondered. The question can be asked again. Was it meant to be that I went farming? At the end of the day does it matter? Because I did. I went farming.

I suppose as a Mennonite it was in my genes to be a farmer and/or a preacher. Although less so in my generation, venturing out into the world to get a higher education or pursue other ambitions were not always encouraged. I sometimes wonder whether I made life choices because I had been socialized a certain way or because I simply didn't have the chutzpah to even think about pursuing anything else.

I do find it interesting that my father seemed to experience life in a similar way. He grew up on a farm, began farming at a young age, became a pastor while he was farming, but always seemed to have other interests as well. To the point where he did further his education, sold the farm, and began a whole new career. I wish he had lived longer so I could have had that conversation with him when I was grappling with my own life choices. I think it might have clarified my own choices and decisions.

I grew up on a turkey and grain farm. Although I was involved in daily chores, working in the fields, and other farm jobs, farming just never seemed to be part of who I was and who I wanted to be. Then again, I am not convinced that I ever gave much thought to my future. Whether it was my parents not providing enough direction or me just being a lazy sort, I kind of cruised through my high school years with no plans. None of this "when I grow up I want to be . . . ."

After graduating from high school, with marks just barely above passing, I set out to explore the world. That may be overstating it just a bit. However, I did leave home to join two friends in a construction business. That lasted all of a year before we all went our separate ways. Although I did not realize it at the time, one of those friends had some reservations about carrying on with that business.

Some thirty-five years after the fact, we were sitting around having pizza with friends. I suspect we must have been reminiscing when my wife looked at the one friend and asked why that construction business did not carry on. Without missing a beat, suggesting that this had been thought through on more than one occasion, he explained that he had not had confidence that we could succeed. During a week that fall, he was sick, and when he came back to the job, he claimed my co-worker and I had only managed to put up two sheets of plywood. (In certain Mennonite circles I am now called twei toffle Friese. A direct English translation is two-sheets Friesen.) That may be closer to the truth than I care to think about. Having said that, I suspect had the construction business carried on it would probably have resulted in a similar end game as my farming attempt. Based on the careers we both ended up in, it's obvious that our skills were much better served in other areas.

After that year of construction, I was left looking for other employment. Jobless and not able to afford the basics of life, I had to move back in with my parents. As I reflect on the jobs I applied for, I now realize I still had not figured out what I wanted to be

Chapter 2 Was I a Farmer? An Identity Crisis

when I grew up. I did meet the qualifications for selling pots and pans door to door, but that just did not seem appealing. I ended up becoming an assistant manager of a clothing store in southeastern Manitoba.

As I found out after the fact, the reason I got the job was because I kept phoning and asking the manager about the job. He suggested that meant I was driven to do that work whereas I knew I was desperate. Surely I had found a new career path. Because I knew that town's mother tongue (low German), I was quite adept at selling suits in either German or English. It wasn't hard work physically and, by no means, mentally challenging. It was only a matter of months before I realized that my paycheque barely covered my monthly gas bill. Although I was fortunate to be living rent-free with my parents, I needed to move out and move on. I needed a job that was more physically demanding and paid better.

For three years, I enjoyed the experience of working for a building mover. The company was owned by a father, his son, and son-in-law. It was the son that hired me, so for the most part that was who I worked with. However, his dad would occasionally do some jobs and would pick workers from the other crews to help him. Let me rephrase that. Someone would be designated to work with him. You see, working with him was a challenge. He was a gruff man, set in his ways and so not always pleasant to be around. In later years, I came to understand that underneath all the gruffness was a man with a softer, kinder demeanour. For a twenty-year-old, that was not normally visible on the jobsite. Having the least amount of seniority, I would invariably draw the short straw.

One summer we were moving buildings up to Matheson Island, a remote community located in central Manitoba. As you can well imagine, amenities were basically nonexistent. We would buy our food at a grocery store. We stayed the night in a private home, which meant we shared a bedroom. I could talk about the snoring I heard but won't go there—apparently, I do that too. One day I

19

decided that I was going to have a real attitude, talk back, and just seem grouchy myself hoping that he would not want to ever work with me again. As we sat in the truck one noon hour eating, not sure what, but it certainly did not qualify for any of the major food groups, I said something in a gruff and less than respectful way to him. He looked at me with a smile and expressed how much he liked working with me. So much for that strategy.

There is something else I often think of when I think about that gentleman. In the year before my move back to the farm, I had pneumonia twice and bronchitis three times. No doctor could ever explain why. When that boss found out that I was quitting to go hog farming he called me into his office and in the kindest, most gentle way, suggested that, with my lung issues, working in a hog barn would not be helpful and that I should probably reconsider that decision. Perhaps I should have listened to him.

But all this wandering out in the world was not for naught. That four-year stint away from Wawanesa saw another significant event in my life. It so happened I met a girl who would end up becoming a life partner.

A friend of mine and I used to drive into Winnipeg to play pool or drink beer or both. His girlfriend lived with a cousin. One night he needed to stop in at their apartment, so I accompanied him. When we walked in there was a cute girl wearing a cuter hat, sewing something. If I had the ability to paint a picture, I could still paint that one from memory. She was sitting at the sewing machine wearing something that could only be described as a cross between a durag and a cap. She proceeded to tell us a story of how she had wanted to drive to Steinbach from their apartment in South Winnipeg and ended up some twenty-five miles away, in Anola, completely lost. Perhaps the attraction was that here was someone I could help in finding her way. To this day I chuckle when she gives other people directions.

Chapter 2   Was I a Farmer? An Identity Crisis

A few short days later, my friend suggested I ask her out on a date. With shaking knees, I called from a payphone at the Pony Corral restaurant on Pembina Highway, just a few short blocks from her apartment. Thankfully she said yes. My friend and I planned a double date. First, we would attend a Winnipeg Blue Bomber game, then go out for dinner, and end the evening at a bowling alley. The only issue I had is that I could not afford the seventy-five bucks that it was going to cost me. Thankfully my friend had the wherewithal to finance that date for me.

I would like to say the rest is history, but I had some work left to do. Whether it made sense or not, asking parents for their daughter's hand in marriage was a key component in the culture I was from. Clearly that would involve some planning. The timing had to be right: her parents would both have to be home, my girlfriend would have to be away, and hopefully not too many family members around. Ultimately, I decided that I would buy a watermelon for them, wait for when my girlfriend wasn't home, and innocently deliver the watermelon. Long story short they said yes. To her dying day I believe my mother-in-law started giggling every time that or any watermelon came up in conversation.

We got married in late fall of 1981. One evening, a month or two before the wedding, we were chatting about the planning process. My soon-to-be wife was telling me how busy she was. I glibly said to her that I should get hurt at work and go on workers compensation so I could help her. I don't know of anyone that would want to help with wedding planning and get hurt to do it. Furthermore, I am not sure I know of many women that would actually like to have their boyfriends around when they are planning their wedding.

The following day we were moving a house in southeastern Manitoba. For the most part, the houses we moved would be set on basements, and so most of our work would be done inside the basement. This particular house was going on top of a crawl space, meaning we had to lower it by working on the outside. The raising and lowering of houses was done with a series of hydraulic jacks hooked up to a central pumper. As the house got closer to its foundation, I needed to push the hydraulic jacks and hoses through the small gap between the house and the foundation. As I pushed the jack through the narrow opening, a tap on the jack opened, releasing the pressure on the jacks holding up the house. In what felt like slow motion, but clearly wasn't, the house settled down on the foundation, pinning my arm. I let loose with a blood curdling scream. Thankfully my boss was quick to assess the situation, started the pumper, which pressurized the hoses and lifted the house. That quick action saved my arm, but it got squashed enough that I had a month off work. I guess you really need to be careful what you ask for.

As I mentioned earlier, I grew up on a grain and turkey farm. Turkey production in Canada is controlled by a system known as "supply management." That simply means you're allotted a quota by the provincial government that dictates how much you can produce. While still in high school, I had applied for quota. At the time, the province was looking at expanding production and my brother did get some. So, when early in our dating life, I received a letter from the Manitoba Turkey Board saying I was in line for a turkey quota, I was excited. I rushed over to my girlfriend's to show her. I was convinced that it was only a matter of time, and I would have the opportunity to be a turkey farmer. I suppose that was when we started thinking about our future and where we might end up. Ironically enough, as much as that letter provided certain expectations, I never did get any quota.

In spite of that, I often wonder about what was driving me at the time. I was still uncertain about any career. Perhaps it was an escape from something. Was it the job I was in at the time? Or was it some fantasy of a better life that lured us in that direction? Maybe I missed the community I had been part of for the majority

Chapter 2   Was I a Farmer? An Identity Crisis

of my life. And perhaps we were simply being adventurous. By all appearances, it seems I was either suffering from an identity crisis or had never established an identity.

Takeaway

Over the years, as I have dealt with innumerable farm families, I have come to understand the unique identity that farmers have. There is a mindset there not normally seen in many other occupations. There is a connection to the soil they cultivate or the animals they feed. Core values and beliefs are foundational to that identity.

When that connection, those core values or beliefs, are threatened, an identity crisis is unavoidable. That crisis creates uncertainty and confusion. It makes people question who they are and forces them to re-evaluate their values and beliefs and where they fit into the world. It means that they have to figure out who they will be in the next phase of their life and what that may look like.

Because that crisis creates uncertainty, values and beliefs are fluid. It creates a paralysis, a fear of making reasonable decisions. Often the crisis comes with feelings of failure which adds another blow to a fragile self-esteem.

Over time, farming and being a famer has also come with some labels applied by society. That means that behaviours may be influenced by the way society describes or classifies farmers. Over that same time farming has gone through some dramatic changes so that many of those labels don't fit anymore. As much as farming used to be a way of life, it has become much more business oriented.

When I was dealing with farmers in debt mediation, I often heard, "But what will I do if I can't farm?" One evening during our counsellor training, I expressed frustration to the group that farmers I was trying to help kept using that phrase. As I was talking, I looked over to my wife and saw she was smiling. On our way home, I asked her why that had made her smile. She reminded me that I had often used that statement as well. It is a go-to sentiment when faced with financial struggles. Although a change may be inevitable, it is difficult to envision anything past the current crisis.

In most cases it didn't mean the end of farming for my clients, but because of the uncertainty it felt to them like it might be. It is easy to lose sight of the opportunities of the future. We get lost in that identity and are unable to build a new one. That leads to internalizing false expectations. It gets in the way of self-discovery. It keeps us from identifying supports and finding solutions to move on.

Having an identity is important. It gives us a sense of belonging. It improves our wellbeing. It helps in fitting in with others whose identities are like ours. It plays a major role in how we understand and experience our life and work. It helps in having better connections with others.

When our identity is threatened it can become a personal crisis. It's important to face your identity crisis head-on. Don't try to hide from your self-discovery or avoid thinking about it. Don't fall into bad coping strategies or destructive behaviours. Talk about what is important for you, whether that is with family, friends, or even a professional. Only when you face it directly can you move on to the next phase of your life. Through acceptance, you are opening your world to new possibilities, a new stage in your personal development.

In the past I often viewed my farming career as a failure. I had to find ways of getting past that. We have to accept that failure may well come when we try something new. If we let that be our identity, we will lose the ability to move forward.

It needs to be a learning process to educate and get better. We must be willing to dust ourselves off, stand up, and make another attempt. Use your understanding and knowledge of failure to build a foundation from which you can grow, flourish, and maintain perspective. The key is not to be spooked by failure, but rather to have a willingness to fail again, because if we don't take risks, if we don't step outside of our comfort zone, we will not become better. And, most important of all, we must forgive ourselves for the failure. Without forgiveness we will continue to beat ourselves up, which inevitably will lead to more failures without the reward of establishing a true identity.

Chapter 3
Relationships are Important: A Significant Other

I am filled with a peculiar apprehension. As part of telling my story of farming and experiencing mental illness, I felt it was important to ask my wife what impact my mental illness had had on her. When I asked her the question, she said she would need to think about it. One evening she asked whether I wanted to hear her answer. As much as I had asked the question, I was somewhat nervous about hearing the answer. She told me she felt like she had been married to four different men. As much as that statement made me curious, I wasn't sure I wanted to hear anymore.

The first two years of our marriage were fun. We both had good jobs with relatively regular hours. We were involved in a church community, had many wonderful friends, and family was close. However, relationships come with certain expectations. After we got married, I discovered that my wife assumed that I would have the ability to fix things when they broke down. After all, that's what her father had done. That notion was tested early. One day I came home from work and was promptly told the furnace wasn't working, with a tone that suggested that she

Chapter 3   Relationships are Important: A Significant Other

expected me to fix it. Not knowing what I could do about it, but not letting on, I bravely ventured downstairs to see what I could do. Completely baffled by how those things work, I gave it a swift kick. Still don't know what was wrong with it, but whatever it was, that kick fixed it.

Carpentry came much easier for me. The second year we were married, we bought a house trailer, moved it to a quaint little lot and enjoyed life. When the roof sprung a leak in a torrential downpour, I could fix that. I built a nice little deck in the backyard. Fixing cars was a different story. But I was okay as long as we stayed living where we were. My wife's dad and her brother were mechanics, and they had a repair shop just up the street.

Farming did teach me a lot about fixing things when they broke down. I learned about electricity. And sometimes a good shock would teach me to turn off breakers before attempting to change switches or fan motors. I found out how to do plumbing jobs. I was regularly fixing feeding systems and manure scrapers. I figured out how to start tractors by using a screwdriver on the starter. Even found out one day that it's a good idea to make sure it's out of gear. I became self-sufficient in repairs, much to the delight of my wife. I could fix everything, except cars. I still can't fix cars.

As much as my wife might have had certain expectations I suppose, in all honesty, I did as well. That hit home one evening shortly after we got married. The entrance to our house led right into the kitchen and eating area. As I walked through the door after work, I saw that she was busy preparing supper. What I saw frightened me and was not something conducive to calming my hunger pangs. She had prepared a pot of boiled rice to go with the chicken teriyaki she had made. That was something that never would have happened in our home growing up. If we had rice, it would be in the form of a rice pudding with sugar and raisins. But a side to the main entrée? Never. As she tells it, the look in my eyes gave away my true feelings.

My wife is considerably more adventurous with cooking than my mother was. And, for the most part, I have grown to appreciate that. I have grown to like rice as a side to an entrée. She will insist I need more vegetables with my meals. She will challenge me to eat healthfully. And I do try. I have learned to like cucumber salad. I will eat butter chicken. I even try veggies like broccoli, although I still prefer peas or corn. But please, mushrooms? The smell alone is enough to wonder how anyone could eat those. So no, I do not eat mushrooms.

The move to the farm was significantly more of a challenge for her than it was for me. I was simply moving back to a farm and community where I had grown up. She was leaving her community, friends, and family. That, in itself, was a major adjustment.

In addition, my focus became the farm, so she was often left to fend for herself. Shortly after our move, she was offered a manager's job in a grocery store in our local town. She had some experience working in a store, so she accepted that opportunity with excitement. It was interesting to see how quickly she became part of the community and got to know many of the local folks.

Obviously, it was exciting for us when we found out she was pregnant. We looked forward to welcoming our first child. Before we were ready to make that news public, we attended a family get-together at my parents' place. As we were enjoying the meal, my oldest brother informed the family that they were expecting their second child. My other brother, the one I was farming with, then told us that they too, were expecting their second child. I gave my wife a look, she nodded, so I proceeded to let everyone know that we were also expecting. That excitement turned to complete devastation when my wife had a miscarriage shortly after.

But it didn't take long, and we were expecting again. It was exciting to welcome our first son into the world in January of 1986. To add to the excitement, we had the New Year's baby for

Chapter 3   Relationships are Important: A Significant Other

our community. As it turns out, that was merely the beginning of our excitement.

What felt like a few short months after the birth, we found out my wife was pregnant again. And in January of 1987 along came our second son. And again, we had the community's New Year's baby. I felt somewhat sheepish when we were leaving the hospital and the nurses said, "See you next year." Just so you know, they didn't. It took *two* years before they saw us again.

With the first two being so close in age, we knew if we wanted more children, that should happen sooner than later. We agreed that we would try for a third child and two years later it happened. We just missed having the New Year's baby for that year.

I had always hoped that the third one would be a girl to provide some balance. The day she was born, my wife—and she clearly had some experience by now—knew the birth was imminent. However, the doctor wasn't so sure, thinking he would have time to go home for supper and come back later. But when my wife says something will happen, it usually does. She was still in a regular hospital room when the festivities began. And it happened fast. Through my own panic because of the sounds I was hearing, feeling quite helpless and knowing I should be doing something, but not sure what, and some slight nausea because of what I was seeing, but trying not to, I saw enough to know we had our daughter.

I would at times suggest to people we had done our family planning the right way, although some might argue there didn't seem to be any planning involved. In my mind, having the kids close together would give us the opportunity to have babies, get that over with and then be a family unit that would find similar interests as we navigated life.

The thought was good, reality not so much. Again, it made for a steep learning curve and lots of work. As you can well imagine, having a baby and being pregnant made life quite challenging for my wife. When I wasn't busy on the farm, I would spend time with our newborn and probably wasn't aware enough of what she was experiencing. When our second son came along, I thought it would be more of the same. What worked for the first one surely would work with the second one. I found out quickly that was not the case. And then along came our daughter and everything changed again.

Shortly after our kids were born, my life changed drastically. My off-farm work was getting busier. I was often away from home for nights on end. That left the bulk of parenting to my wife. It was also during that time when life and work would overwhelm me, and my coping skills were not conducive to healthy relationships. My wife managed to juggle parenthood and supporting, as best she could, a husband who was quickly losing his way. Although at times frustrating, she has a stubbornness to her which served us well during those years.

It was many years later, when I began talking publicly about my mental health, that she talked about the "different" husbands she had experienced. They were all me!

The first two years we were a young couple working together on building a life. It was a time of learning together, building a home, and enjoying everything that comes with being newlyweds.

Then we went farming, and along came husband number two. My focus changed. I jumped into a partnership with my brother. I seemed to forget my relationship with a relatively new wife and focused on a relationship with my brother and all that came with building a business.

When the stressors of life took control, my coping methods were not healthy, and I became the third husband, someone she wished she wasn't married to. My personality changed. I withdrew from the important aspects of life. That led to an addiction issue that wreaked havoc on our relationship.

It is no secret that trust is the very foundation that relationships are built on. Without trust, relationships cannot grow and flourish. It should come as no surprise that during those times in

Chapter 3 Relationships are Important: A Significant Other

my life when I was not the husband she had married, trust was an issue. In retrospect that makes sense. How does one trust a person who can hardly function as a human being never mind being a responsible husband and father? Through those experiences, she had to make significant adjustments.

As our kids were quite young when I was going through those dark times, I was always convinced that they wouldn't have noticed. But I was wrong. My kids have shared with me about crying themselves to sleep because of their concern over their father and our financial issues. They related how they had stood at the top of the stairs and listened as their mother and I talked about my mental health. They were there when I struggled with my coping skills. I had no idea the degree to which this had impacted them. And perhaps it was better, because I suspect had I known, the guilt and shame might well have pushed me over the edge.

It was only after I addressed my mental health and addictions that I became husband number four, someone she could appreciate as a partner. That involved taking responsibility for my actions. I had to be proactive with healing from the past and working towards mental wellness.

As much as my wife talks about being married to two men she didn't particularly care for, and I know it's not a laughing matter, I do sometimes suggest she is the one that picked me to be her husband.

Some time ago, I picked her up from work. As we were driving home, we were catching up on the day that had been. Suddenly she became rather serious and said she needed to share something with me.

My immediate concern began to rise with her seriousness. I racked my brain, wondering if I had done something wrong or if she had. I couldn't bear the suspense and finally asked her what was on her mind.

She looked at me and informed me that a man she knew before she met me had passed away. Why in the world would that even matter to me? It took a moment, but then the reality hit me. Of all the men she had gone out with before marrying me, this was the last one to pass away. Sadly, they all departed this world at much too early an age. As you can imagine, this revelation got me thinking. I did briefly wonder how she learned of his death, but I decided to let that question slide.

My mind was preoccupied with a more significant concern. I knew I had to dig deeper into this, but I wasn't entirely sure I wanted to uncover the truth. Had I narrowly escaped some ill-fated destiny? My main worry was whether I was still a work in progress and if I should start sleeping with one eye open.

For numerous years, we lived in the farmhouse that I had grown up in. We had sometimes planned on renovating that house, but, due to circumstances, that didn't work out. We then decided that we would build a house away from the farm. All of us were excited about the prospect of a new place to call our own. The lot overlooked a valley and the kids saw new opportunities for exploring. We spent hours poring over house plans to find something that worked for us but would also fit in at our unique location. In addition to that, we decided to do our own general contracting, which meant we really needed to work together.

It has sometimes been suggested that building a house is one of the greatest relational stressors a couple can experience. The night prior to the start of construction, I told my wife that we should make sure we kissed each other goodnight every night, just to make sure all was good. That lasted a week, and we haven't kissed since. Okay, that's not entirely true, but it did take a concerted effort for open communication and working together for that project to be completely successful.

I really think, and my wife might disagree, that travelling in a vehicle creates the most tension between us. Okay, so do self-checkouts, but I am leaving that one alone. The driving tension comes from a combination of two things. First, she is a cautious driver and by

Chapter 3   Relationships are Important: A Significant Other

extension a nervous passenger. Secondly, I have very little patience for other drivers. She has at times, as a passenger, questioned my conflict management skills.

Recently, as we ventured out on the highways and byways of Manitoba, snow began to fall. As happens, there was snow drifting across the road and some was accumulating on the sides of the asphalt. In essence, normal winter driving. However, my wife being a worrywart about all things related to winter driving, was quite nervous. I tried. I really did. Drove somewhat slower than I usually drive. Was careful when meeting oncoming traffic. Didn't pass people even when they were driving much slower than necessary. Just really thought I was being considerate, certainly more so than the people driving too slowly.

As luck would have it, I ventured too far to the right and the front tire slipped off the pavement onto the shoulder. No harm done other than the heart attack my wife was having. Along with that, I also heard some strange noises coming out of her mouth. I suspect she was saying bad words about me. I asked what the problem was, and she replied that she had known before we even left home that this would happen. Talk about foresight!

In all my wisdom I said, "it happened, but nothing happened". I thought about that and repeated it and suggested what a brilliant quote that was. At the time she didn't seem convinced.

The more I thought about it, the more I realized how important that quote is for life in general. How often have I and do I worry and ruminate about future events. I am concerned over how things will turn out. I lose sleep thinking about all the worst things that will come of whatever it is that I am worrying about. And it seems that the more stress I have the more I worry and stew.

But most times, when I rethink an event that has happened and that I was concerned about, I realize that *nothing happened*. I survived and things turned out better than expected. Reminded me again of a story told about Winston Churchill. A friend of his, lying on his death bed, said that he had had a lot of trouble in life, most of which never happened. There is a lesson here. It happened, but nothing happened.

When my wife and I chat about what might have been, particularly as it concerns our decision to go farming, she often reminds me that raising our kids on the farm was worth it all. Our kids have innumerable fond memories of that farm. The valleys, creeks and rivers surrounding our farm provided for countless hours of exploring and adventure. Swimming, fishing, hiking, and exploring never got boring. We built forts and treehouses. We had wiener roasts. We went tobogganing.

Of particular note are memories of when our friends, with their similarly aged kids, would come for visits. Often a visit with them turned into us trying to recreate our childhood. Perhaps not recreating as much as showing our kids the many things we had done when we were young.

During my childhood, I always had a strong desire to own a dirt bike, a snowmobile, or a go-cart. Unfortunately, this dream never became a reality. The financial means to purchase such toys were simply not available during my youth. In hindsight, I now understand that my parents had different priorities. They had a deep appreciation for travel and camping, and as a result, we did a lot of that.

As my own children reached an age where they wanted motorized toys, I decided to fulfill a part of my childhood dream by buying a Honda Odyssey. In a way, it was like living vicariously through them. The Honda Odyssey, essentially a souped-up go-cart, provided a great deal of enjoyment when it actually worked. Regrettably, it demanded an abundance of maintenance and repairs, skills I sorely lacked. Consequently, I eventually decided to part with it.

A few years later, I made the choice to buy a snowmobile. To my chagrin, this purchase didn't fare much better. Starting it was often a daunting task and keeping it running proved to be a significant challenge. Frustration eventually got the best of me, and I

Chapter 3 Relationships are Important: A Significant Other

informed my kids that I would provide them with something that required no mechanical expertise. They got a trampoline.

I frequently remind my children that while we might not have possessed all the toys that many of their friends did, they had a unique opportunity in the form of our travels. Whether through my work or other means, we embarked on numerous family journeys. Perhaps this is a clear indicator that I inherited more of my parents' values than I initially realized.

Takeaway

There's a certain magic that occurs when two souls connect and discover compatibility. Together, we bring children into the world, nurturing them with deep love and care. We form bonds with friends, sharing both joyous moments and hardships. To maintain these relationships takes effort.

Life presents a myriad of challenges, but maintaining healthy, close relationships is crucial for overcoming them and leading a fulfilling life. These relationships act as a safeguard against isolation, loneliness, depression, and unsafe behaviors. They require ongoing maintenance and effort to remain fulfilling and positive. Otherwise they can become sources of stress and unhappiness. The closer our connections to loved ones, the more we experience positive mental health and overall well-being.

Relationships are fundamental to our existence. Many years ago, I encountered a quote in a hair salon that resonated deeply: "Relationships provide us with identity, purpose, and direction. In essence, relationships and therefore community are a life-giving, life-defining, life-nurturing process."

Establishing connections based on trust is crucial. Trust is built by practicing openness and transparency. Fundamentally, trust is nurtured through embracing vulnerability on an emotional level. This enables us to openly communicate our weaknesses, errors, and fears, fostering adaptability, understanding, and collective growth.

Being involved with others, being able to trust others, requires us to be authentic. And to be authentic requires us to become vulnerable, to open ourselves up. That is a frightening thought. We have a tendency to hide behind walls. We are alarmed at the thought of others finding out who we really are. But when we practice vulnerability, we see ourselves and others in a different light. It opens up a whole new world.

Relationships require open and honest communication and a real desire to understand the other person. When we communicate, when we show others the willingness to listen and understand, we are working positively on our relationship.

Failure to communicate leaves us in the dark about the lives of those we love, resulting in feelings of hurt and rejection. It's essential to remain curious, open-minded, and willing to explore when we encounter behaviors or statements we don't immediately understand.

At the heart of every relationship lies the desire to be understood. Understanding and being understood are facilitated by empathy, compassion, and warmth in our interactions. You will be surprised at the warm feeling you get when you are able to share what you are thinking, when you listen to what the other is saying and when both of you seek to understand.

Be aware of who you are and the role you play in relationships. Understand your trigger points, those things in life that have a tendency to set you off. Be open about your shortcomings and build on the strengths you bring to the relationship. Interpersonal relationships are an essential part of a happy and productive life.

If we build on relationships, when we share with each other, when we talk, we gain the freedom we so desperately strive for. We discover a world we knew could exist but couldn't see. That defines us. That gives us direction. That gives us purpose.

Chapter 4
What Have I Done? The Reality Hits Hard

I am scared, frightened beyond belief. The reality of my situation hits like a polar vortex in the midst of a spring thaw. It doesn't feel right. The idyllic allure of being a farmer is quickly disappearing in the fumes rising to meet me. I am trying desperately to keep the sludge moving in the right direction. Pigs are nipping at my legs. The air is thick with ammonia. As I jump from one pen to the next, pigs running through the moving manure sends it flying everywhere. I keep my mouth firmly closed to avoid eating it, and my glasses are covered. It is soaking through my coveralls. In that moment, I confront the truth. I know this was not what I had bargained for. I want out.

Wanting to go back to the farm came with a challenge. My father and my brother each had turkey quotas. That meant that for me to become part of the family farm, we would need to diversify. Growing up I had always known that I would not want to be a hog producer. My uncle had a hog barn right across the road from our farm. The sounds and smells coming from there did nothing to entice me to that type of farming. When my father wanted to leave the farm, it opened an opportunity for me. However, to expand the farm to support two families, it seemed to be a given that we would get into hog production.

That first winter was enjoyable. Because of my carpentry experience, we felt we could do the barn construction ourselves. We designed the barn as it was being constructed. There was a certain novelty to it. We hired a cousin and between him, my brother, and me we built the barn. Any challenges that came along were easily dealt with. And by spring it was ready for hogs.

Just as construction was wrapping up, two of my aunts came to pay a visit. They wanted to see firsthand what we had been up to all winter. We gave them the grand tour of the new barn. A short time later I heard that one of my aunts had made a comment to my mother about how unhappy I had appeared.

That struck me. At the time I was not convinced that I was unhappy. Looking back, this may already have been an indication of what was to come with my mental health. As we came closer to buying our first pigs, I remember wondering exactly what I had got myself into. However, being young and having moved from job to job, never staying long in one place, I went with the flow. Perhaps still looking for that magic that I thought would be just over the next hill. I attacked my new role with vigour, the same vigour that provided the energy to build the barn, young enough not to back off from any challenges.

Part of our mentality at the time was that we were not afraid of hard work, so the barn was designed in the simplest way. Normally hog barns are built with manure pits under the pens. But we did things differently. We built the barn with an open gutter concept as that saved significant money. Physical work did not concern us, so scraping manure manually and shovelling feed did not scare us. Little did we know.

It was exciting when the first pigs arrived. The barn was new and clean. In an effort to make the pigs comfortable when they arrived, we

Chapter 4 What Have I Done? The Reality Hits Hard

had put some wood shavings in each pen. It even smelled welcoming in there. And then everything changed. In less than a day, what had been a clean, fresh-smelling barn was now filled with grunting, stinky pigs. The air was suffocating. The pigs were dirty. Surely something had gone drastically wrong. Adjustments had to be made. Knowing very little about raising livestock, learning came by trial and error.

So began my new reality. Manually filling feeders, which meant shovelling two tonnes of feed daily, but at least it could be done without the interference from pigs. Scraping manure morning and evening and sometimes in between. This was somewhat more arduous. Jumping from pen to pen, having pigs nipping at my legs, trying to keep the liquid manure moving in the right direction, and inhaling the gasses that are released when manure is stirred very quickly took away the glamour of my new life.

I suppose, in a sense, the physical labour did have some benefits. After having scraped manure and shovelling feed for a few months, I had lost significant weight and gained substantial muscle. I will never forget the day I attended an event at the local high school. As I walked into the gym, I spied the peg board, a contraption on the wall that you climbed using your arms and pegs. That was something I hadn't even thought of trying when I went to school. It would have been much too embarrassing, and I probably would have hurt myself, but now it was piquing my curiosity. I sauntered over, gave it a try, and was pleasantly surprised how easy it was.

However, all that work was not what I had bargained for. I began wondering how I could escape this hell I was in. I suspect the glamour of being a farmer had now been replaced with the reality of the rest of my life. The only way out was to die. I had made a commitment to farm and was of the thought, though not suicidal, that death was the only way out. I will never forget, as I scraped manure, thinking that getting lung cancer and dying was the only way.

To this day I am not sure why I picked lung cancer. Surely there would be simpler and easier ways of dying. I suppose that I was thinking lung cancer because my grandmother had died from that, and I had struggled with smoking on and off. I had always been told that lung cancer was genetic and so maybe, in my mind, I had a good start to getting cancer. I now live with COPD, a lung condition normally associated with smoking. My doctor says it's because I used to smoke. I keep trying to convince him it is "farmer lung," due to working in a barn for all those years. Not sure it makes a difference. And perhaps it's a little of both.

The feed company my father and brother had dealt with for years was excited to see us building a hog barn. They had just developed a new hog feeding program which they thought would be just right for us. As it turns out, it was far from just right.

For a number of months, we dealt with various issues. The mortality rate of our hogs was too high but always attributed to certain disease concerns. Then we brought in a batch of weanlings from a different genetic source. Within a few weeks, I noticed that some of the pigs were physically deteriorating. Too many pigs were dying. As much as the pigs were in a comfortable environment, had lots of water and feed, something was off. We decided that we needed to get a vet involved to help us find the problem. So when a pig near market weight died, I decided I needed to take it to the vet clinic.

The previous night had seen significant snowfall, and we had not had a chance to clear the road to the barn. To get a pig to the vet meant I would have to drag the carcass back through the valley to our main yard. The pig was almost market weight, in excess of two hundred pounds, so it clearly took significant effort. When I finally got there, I discovered the truck was gone. That left only one option. My hatchback car. With a lot of grunting, groaning, and maneuvering I managed to load it. The size of the pig meant the head rested on what normally would have been the driver's arm rest.

The postmortem on that pig revealed that it had died due to a gastric ulcer. I had a significant discussion with the vet on what

Chapter 4 What Have I Done? The Reality Hits Hard

could have caused the ulcer. Although the vet did have some ideas, he felt it best to investigate further. That meant taking some live pigs to a lab in Winnipeg so that an in-depth analysis could be carried out.

The postmortems on those pigs confirmed we had an ulcer issue. That meant we had to figure out what was causing the ulcers. It being before the days of internet meant finding and reading significant material on the cause of ulcers and how to fix that issue. It involved doing our own postmortems on the pigs. I found it interesting how adept I became in cutting open dead pigs, doing a cursory view of all major organs, and then pulling out the stomach and finding another ulcer.

We knew that the feeding program we were using was called a high-nutrient density feed, meaning the corn levels were higher than normal. What we learned is that when using high levels of corn, the feed should not be ground as fine as it was. The feed company was not easily convinced that the feed was an issue. They came up with various reasons for the ulcer problem.

And each day that went by we were losing more pigs. It was only after we demanded a change in the feed program that the problems began to ease, and we were able to turn the corner. By that time, we had experienced significant financial losses, something a start-up operation can hardly sustain. In retrospect, it feels like those financial challenges stayed with us through our entire farming experience.

Farming of any sort comes with a unique set of stressors. The World Health Organization has long classified farming as being one of the most stressful occupations. I should have known that but didn't. As with many other things in life, I had jumped in without giving thought to what might be involved.

The feed situation at the outset was but one of numerous problems we had over the years. We dealt with disease issues in our hogs and turkeys. Sourcing a weanling supply was an ongoing challenge.

Equipment breakdowns happened often, not uncommon in livestock operations. But with each challenge that came along, we tried our best to adapt. We worked our way through them.

It is also well known that many stressors are outside the control of farmers. The market price we received for hogs was dictated by supply and demand. That meant there could be significant swings in prices. If there was a glut of production in the North American marketplace, prices would drop. When that glut disappeared prices would increase. That hog supply would fluctuate based on grain production. When crop production yields were good, hog production would increase. And with that variation in crop production, feed prices would also go through dramatic changes. It was all about timing and risk management.

Risk management included watching markets, trying to determine patterns, and locking in prices that could provide for a positive margin. That could be challenging as well, as pricing can fluctuate for various reasons. One day I read a market report that said hog prices had dropped because the American government had imposed import duties on Chinese tires. The Chinese, in turn, investigated whether the US was dumping chicken products into China. That prompted a fear of a chicken glut in the United States that would see retail prices drop for chicken drawing consumers away from pork. In essence, because of an American trade action on tires, the price I was getting for my hogs was negatively impacted.

Many farmers in my generation have a vivid memory of interest rates hitting 20 percent. You can imagine what that did for debt servicing. Most other input costs, such as fuel, hydro, maintenance, and other things, have steadily increased over time. I often found myself thinking that I was producing enough food to feed a small city but was finding it difficult to feed *my* family.

At the same time, there was increased pressure coming from the environmental front. I get that the way things used to be done

Chapter 4 What Have I Done? The Reality Hits Hard

was not acceptable anymore. But at the same time, new legislation was forcing farmers out of business due to prohibitive costs associated with upgrades.

And what was always on the forefront was trade negotiations. On the one hand, freer trade should help with an increase in hog returns. But freer trade meant that supply management was being threatened, which made us question the viability of our turkey operation.

It's easy to get lost in the negative aspects of farming. There is, however, another reality. There is a certain excitement in learning new things. And farming certainly provides opportunities for that. Just as I had learned new skills in the work I did prior to farming, I had the chance to learn many new ones as a farmer.

Although situations like the ulcer problem in our pigs can be devastating, there were times when we could feel proud of our accomplishments. With each challenge that came along, we figured things out. We adapted. We learned new management tricks. And when things worked out, there was a sense of accomplishment.

I was able to attend meetings, seminars, and agricultural shows. I met countless other producers and industry folks. Doing business with agricultural companies is a unique experience. Relationships are built with service providers. It is a personal touch not easily experienced in other areas of life.

Living on a farm also meant being part of a rural community. Many of those are tight-knit communities where everyone knows everyone. When you met someone on the road, and they didn't wave, you knew they were a stranger to those parts. If it was someone you knew, and they didn't wave, you were tempted to turn around and follow them, check in and make sure they were okay. When you went into a local business you never left without chatting about something other than what you were there for. And you always knew that the coffee shop would be welcoming and there would be others to share stories with. The rural community provided unique opportunities for connection.

Although times are changing, farming for me was more than just a business. It was a lifestyle. It meant I was my own boss. If my kids had a hockey tournament, I could adjust my work schedule so I could attend those games. When my wife wanted me to go shopping with her, it was easy for me to accommodate that. Sure, these things sometimes meant that I would work late in the evenings or on weekends, but that was okay.

Raising our kids on the farm also provided for some training moments. We all know of businesses that prefer hiring young people who were farm kids. That clearly is an indication of a work ethic learned, as well as the knowledge gained by all things farming. It gave our kids some real-life work experience. I have seen them utilize that experience in later years when they got their own places to live. So, if a water pump created issues or a fence needed building or a vehicle broke down, they had the basic knowledge to get things done.

Takeaway

We have all heard that what doesn't kill us makes us stronger. I often have serious questions about that. At first blush it makes sense. After all, we all have challenges in life. We have experiences that we would rather not have. Usually we learn from these experiences, we grow, we do become stronger. But not always.

Some events, some experiences, some trauma will test the very core of our strength and will leave us weakened. And when we get kneecapped by something that weakens us, we must find ways to recover and heal, understanding that we may never recover our former strength.

I chatted recently with an elderly lady who had shown amazing strength and resilience through adversity and pain. As we addressed

Chapter 4 What Have I Done? The Reality Hits Hard

her latest challenge, I made a comment about that strength. She looked at me with a weary gaze and said she was getting tired of being strong. Ongoing challenges, pain, and frustration had left her tired.

And often when we are in situations that require ongoing strength, we do become weary. We become jaded. Our perception gets thrown for a loop. And when that happens, we begin to reflect on the past and feel that life has been a waste. Then feelings of regret take over and we think woulda, shoulda, coulda—the holy trinity of regrets.

Let me use another analogy. The rearview mirror on our cars is small. How successful are we in moving forward if we only look at that small mirror? Even the warning "objects may be closer than they appear" holds some truth. Sometimes the past seems to be sneaking up on us and comes close enough to create worry but ultimately need not be a problem unless we are backing up. However, when we look ahead through the windshield, we have a significantly better view of all the opportunities that await us.

To keep moving forward, use the windshield and accept the future for all it has to offer. We may fail and we may think we wasted part or all of our life. Use the understanding and knowledge of the failure to build a foundation. From this foundation, you can grow, flourish, and maintain perspective.

In a conversation with a friend about recovering, she concluded her thoughts by saying that to recover is to let go of all our losses while not forgetting about the positives. It is far too easy to focus on the negatives. I had serious doubts when the reality of farming hit. But I now have a choice. Do I think about all the bad that happened, or do I reflect on all the good I experienced? I know I am a lot happier when I relive the good memories. Whether you're the praying type or not, the following sums it up best when reality hits hard.

God, grant me the serenity to accept the things I cannot change, the courage to change the things I can, and the wisdom to know the difference.

CHAPTER 5
The Hatchet Twins: Partners in Crime

On a brisk fall evening, my brother and I find ourselves huddled beneath our manure truck. The wind is frigid, seeping through our clothing and chilling us to the bone. As is often the case on a farm, the truck has decided to break down. It was badly needed so we were determined to get it back in operation. Working by the fading light, we huddle together, sharing glances of uncertainty, and chuckling at our collective lack of mechanical expertise. It is a test of patience and teamwork as we figure out where each piece and bolt need to go. We manage to put pieces back in their place, hold our breath, start the engine, and the truck roars back to life. Together we overcame the challenge and got the job done.

It was curious ending up farming with a brother, five years my senior. We were not close growing up. In fact, any type of interaction we had was somewhat awkward. Yet, as we matured into young adults, a bond began to form. So in early 1983 when my brother broached the idea of buying our father's farm and expanding it, I jumped at the opportunity.

Chapter 5 The Hatchet Twins: Partners in Crime

Our looks were so similar that people often mistook us for twins. During winters we used to have beards. One winter I had one, but my brother did not. One night, after our young kids had gone to bed, I shaved the beard. The following morning, before we got out of bed, the kids came running into our bedroom. As soon as they saw me, they stopped in horror. They asked their mother why she was in bed with their uncle.

Although we were brothers, and looked it, we had different approaches to life. Our personalities were different. We had different goals. Our approach to relationships was different. As with animal husbandry, and my relatively new marriage, the learning curve for this new relationship was steep as well.

In a sense, our situation made the relationship somewhat simpler. Because we had both turkeys and hogs, each of us took charge of one entity. As is important with familial partnerships, we established certain parameters around the partnership. It was important, for the purposes of maintaining healthy relationships, that our wives should not be involved in our day-to-day business operations.

That, of course, eliminates conflict on the one hand but does create tension on the other. It was difficult, at times, for our wives to observe what was going on and not be able to have input. And, as is common in those partnerships, there was a certain frustration for me when my wife would express concerns, and I felt I was being put between a rock and a hard place.

Particularly in the first years, the work on the farm meant long hours. Any extracurricular activities added to the time I was not spending with my wife and kids. My brother and I enjoyed playing hockey and were part of a team involved in an old timer league of sorts. We made a good defense pairing, fondly referred to as the hatchet twins. We were both avid golfers so went for a round of golf whenever we could. We tried to attend as many hog and turkey meetings as possible in our quest to learn more about our industries.

Any and all relationships also involve conflict. Conflict can be constructive, if approached with the right attitude. It is through constructive conflict that ideas are born and developed. It helps in finding solutions to problems. Constructive conflict helped us in making decisions, not only in day-to-day operations, but also on longer-term plans. But conflict can also become destructive. When competing forces are at work, the outcome can be less than positive.

When two people with opposite styles work together there can be challenges. My brother had a strong, competitive way about him. That meant he was good at negotiating. He would not easily be swayed from his positions. At one point, in a heated discussion, I suggested he was arrogant. He responded by saying he wasn't arrogant; he just had a certain level of abrasive self-confidence. That actually made me smile, it broke the tension, and I left that conversation knowing I had to get me some of that.

His approach was in direct conflict to mine. I was much more of an accommodator, often even becoming an avoider. So you can well imagine how discussions, conversations and business planning could devolve. And there were times when emotions took over and things were said that would have been best left unsaid. But we also had the ability to tell each other exactly how we felt, using strong language, and then an hour later we would go golfing together.

In later years, we would at times talk about our different approaches. His off-farm work involved significant negotiation skills. I, on the other hand, was involved in work that was geared more for consensus building, helping disputing parties reach agreement. Although we were both good at our individual roles, those different approaches needed to be managed, to ensure that

Chapter 5 The Hatchet Twins: Partners in Crime

our relationship and our business decisions were formed to the best of our abilities.

It is no secret that farming comes with a host of stressors and that stressors can and will create tension. Some stressors last for a day, or a week, and sometimes for a season. Some stressors come from things within our control. Normally these stressors can be dealt with in a relatively short order. Some stressors are outside of our control and are much more difficult to accept and deal with. And when stress hangs around too long it becomes debilitating, tensions increase and along with that, destructive conflict becomes more prevalent.

Financial stress is one of those stressors that plays a significant role in agriculture. Over the course of the first fifteen years of farming, particularly with our challenging start, it felt like cash flow was always problematic. Over that time, we also had to make business decisions on when to expand and how best to grow the business.

Part of that planning involved the decision to sell some of our turkey quota. At the time there was a lot of hype about the great opportunities that existed in the hog industry. Secondly, supply management seemed to be under constant scrutiny, and we were unsure of the sustainability of the turkey industry. So, we sold some quota and expanded our hog operation.

The expansion happened in the spring of 1998 and our first hogs from that expansion were ready for market just prior to Christmas. What had happened in the meantime was a significant downturn in hog markets. By the time we were ready to sell those hogs, the price had dropped to $0.19 per pound, the lowest price in the past fifty years. Where we had spent $130, not including overhead costs, to raise a hog, the return when we sold was a mere $34. Over the course of the following year our losses were substantial. Anecdotally, it was reported that hog producers had lost fifteen years' worth of equity. Ironically that is how long we had been in business. In essence it was like starting over.

Thus started our discussions on how to deal with the ongoing and increasing cash flow issues. As you can imagine the tension was creating conflict. Constant phone calls from the bank telling us we were overdrawn. Feed companies were loath to deliver feed as we were not able to pay for the purchases. We had to discuss payment deferrals with our lenders. The pressure was constant and never-ending.

The only way out for us was to inject personal cash. That, of course, involved a conversation with our wives. Because we were avoiding having them involved in our business, the cash injection conversations created tension and conflict. One of them suggested at the time that, perhaps, we needed to sell out. In retrospect I suspect that would have been the prudent thing to do. Although prices did recover to some degree, the following ten years saw the industry go through significant consolidation, as financial challenges persisted.

Being in partnership meant we needed to work together on most of the more major issues. The gastric ulcer issue in our pigs at the outset, the price crash of '98, production issues that arose due to disease or feed issues, along with others, really put a test to our relationship. We worked together when we purchased a turkey operation and needed to move the building and equipment to our farm. When we expanded our hog facility, we did the construction ourselves. Even more minor issues, like the manure tanker repair mentioned at the beginning, were much better dealt with when we collaborated.

I suspect many looking in from the outside would suggest a lot of the challenges we faced were self-induced. And perhaps so. We were young, ambitious, and energetic. We were always looking to be innovative when it came to our animals, not necessarily going with what was "normally" done. With that kind of focus, some

Chapter 5   The Hatchet Twins: Partners in Crime

things were not important enough to distract us. If it wasn't production related or didn't add to the bottom line, it simply wasn't a priority.

Buying a decent, roadworthy truck was one of those. We had an older truck, which, in essence, was a yard truck. It did also serve as a vehicle to take us to the local coffee shop or into town to pick up supplies, but certainly was not roadworthy enough for any longer trips. For the most part that was all we needed. When longer trips were required, we had our cars.

In late fall of 1984, my brother and I needed to attend to some business in Brandon. Not having our cars available to us we decided to take the old truck. The discussions with the feed company took longer than we had expected and as we stepped outside the weather had changed. There was a significant layer of clouds that had moved in, and sleet had begun to fall. Because of the approaching dusk we knew we might be in a little bit of a dilemma. The old truck did not have functioning taillights and only one, somewhat dim, headlight. To avoid undue traffic or police, we decided we would cut cross country and stick to gravel roads. The intent was good, the result not so much.

On the southern outskirts of Brandon, we turned off the highway. We had a good idea of where we needed to make our next turn. However, due to poor visibility, a mixture of sleet and rain falling on the windshield, and our single headlight, we missed our corner. Being used to grid roads, we were convinced that if we kept going we would eventually get to another corner.

As we kept driving, the road quickly deteriorated into a glorified cow path. However, being good old country boys, we had experienced worse. In the gathering darkness we saw a small rise in the road. As we came to the top of that rise, we hit a small rock that was buried in one of the ruts and blew out a front tire. It being what it was, carrying a spare tire had never crossed our mind.

With little choice, this still being in the pre cellphone era, we began walking, retracing where we had just driven. The rain and sleet were falling, it was dark, and we were not dressed for a hike. We had no idea how far we would need to walk to find a place to phone from. It took some time and as we found out later, we had walked close to seven miles.

Eventually we came across a yard where someone was home. We were able to contact a friend who came to pick us up. When we finally got home, we knew that we still needed to go rescue our truck. We were able to borrow a spare tire from a neighbour who happened to have a similar vehicle and late that night we ventured back.

As we crested that same rise in the glorified cow path, making sure to avoid the rock, we were in for quite a surprise. What we had failed to notice earlier, due to minimal headlights, was that we were within forty feet of driving over a significant drop into the Assiniboine River. The rock creating a blowout, had saved us from much bigger problems, and maybe even saved our lives.

The truth of the matter is there were events that we found ourselves in that could have been avoided by making different decisions. It has sometimes been said that one is always one decision away from a completely different life.

I have spent time reflecting on that. Perhaps life is like that little rock that kept us from plummeting into the Assiniboine River. Sometimes, when we make bad decisions, those rocks are there to save us from tragedy. Initially those rocks create problems. But then, as we found out, those rocks save us from bigger problems. Other times those rocks are not there, and we find ourselves with bigger problems. And when that happens working in partnership with someone else makes for a better life.

Whether self-induced or with things being completely outside of our control, the end became inevitable. By 2005 it had become clear that the farm was not financially sustainable. We needed to

Chapter 5   The Hatchet Twins: Partners in Crime

sell and move on. Aside from the farm just not being sustainable, our off-farm interests had taken over. In a final act of solidarity, we were able to sell the farm and wind down operations. And by Christmas of 2007 that was done.

Takeaway

Being in business with family, can and will provide a variety of challenges. Maintaining familial relationships while dealing with the vagaries of business is not easy and require skills many of us don't come by naturally.

As siblings mature into young adults, relationships mature as well. Sibling rivalry changes to a relationship of equals. It evolves into friendships. Bonds are created. And ultimately, when siblings go into business together a significant paradigm shift must occur. There needs to be a shift from the sibling friendship relationship to a goal of working together in harmony, as partners with a keen awareness and understanding of each other and the business.

Obviously there are various advantages and disadvantages to families working together in business. It is important to identify what they are in a clear, concise, and honest conversation prior to formalizing the relationship as this allows for the establishment of policies which will address future conflicts in the most effective way.

Aside from personality differences, attitudes, perceptions, communication styles, and conflict management styles that exist in any business relationship, the family business relationship has added challenges that come into play. Often those challenges include conflicts that can devolve into sibling rivalries of old, mixed in with new conflicts that arise in businesses. There needs to be a strategy in place for the times when personal matters interfere with business decisions.

Everyone approaches conflict differently but always in the way that makes them feel most comfortable. Humans seem to be wired in a certain way, and it can be challenging to change their approach. However, as you navigate your way through situations that involve relationships, you will find that different scenarios warrant different approaches.

As I alluded to earlier, my brother and I had different approaches. We needed to ensure we were aware of those differences. At times we needed to step away from what we felt comfortable with, avoid being competitive or accommodating, and use a more compromising approach. But ultimately, working collaboratively proved most effective in resolving conflicts in a positive way.

So how can we make it work? There are many families that have succeeded in accomplishing a family first/business first model. That sounds contradictory but isn't. When family members work together, they in essence have two relationships, the one that involves family and the one in business. They are equally important so must be maintained that way. It requires awareness, effective communication strategies, and ongoing conversations. Most of all it requires a desire to build on relationships. It requires the ability to maintain the familial relationship as the business relationship develops.

Chapter 6
This Happened to Me: Farming with Reckless Abandon

I find myself in the pump house for our well. I need to fix the wiring for the pump. Not that I am an electrician, but when it comes to many things on the farm, you learn. The electrical breaker is broken and so it needs replacing. The main breaker is in the barn so, instead of taking the time to go switch it off, I decide to try the repair with live wires. Just as I get the wires close to where they will be connected, they touch the side of the panel, sparks fly, and I feel a weird vibration. As it turns out, the vibrations I felt was my cell phone going off in my shirt pocket. I was sitting in a meeting, had dozed off and the whole episode had been a dream. I jumped and quickly looked around to see if anyone had noticed. Surprisingly I had not uttered a sound.

As can well be imagined, farming brings with it innumerable experiences. We all know accidents happen. Sometimes it's due to carelessness. At times we take too many risks. Other times we get caught up in life and lose focus on the task at hand. The truck story in the last chapter reminded me of a few more experiences I had. I can now look back on some of those experiences and chuckle while others make me shake my head.

There was the night we borrowed, without asking, two tractors. One evening, my brother and his wife in their car and my wife and I in ours, were heading home from a wedding some two hours from home. Although it was only October the weather had turned nasty. It was snowing quite heavily, and the winds were gusty. My brother and his wife followed me as I was quite familiar with the road we were on. Through the blowing snow, I spotted a detour sign. I did not see it well enough to realize it did not apply to our highway, but in a state of panic I turned off the highway and tried to follow an unknown gravel road, hoping to get back to a highway.

That happened to be a day when my car was using more gas than usual. Approximately five miles into a detour that shouldn't have been, my car stalled. It made no sense that I could possibly be out of gas. However, our best guess was that gas is what was needed. Through the blowing snow we spotted a yard light in the distance, so we hopped in my brother's car to go see if we could find some gas.

By now there was a significant accumulation of snow and when we managed to get to the yard, we got hopelessly stuck. As luck would have it, there was nobody home. Trying to think how we could get out of this dilemma, we scouted the yard and came across a tractor in the machine shed. We were able to get it running and used it to push the car back to the road. I sometimes wonder if the folks that lived there ever knew and can imagine their puzzlement as to what had transpired on their yard that day.

Having few options, we finally decided that we would leave our car there as we needed to get home to do our chores. When we did get home our troubles just continued. Because we had not expected the drastic turn in temperatures, nothing had been winterized. Our water pump that supplied water to the hog barn had frozen. So began another battle. We undertook the arduous task of

Chapter 6   This Happened to Me: Farming with Reckless Abandon

pulling the system apart so it could be brought to the barn to be thawed. To do that we needed to bring our truck down to the well. As it turns out, getting to the well was fine. Getting back out was a problem due to a build-up of ice and snow.

By now, it was two o'clock in the morning, and our options were once again limited. The only choice we had was to hike across the road to my uncle's farm and steal his tractor. So that is what we did. It all worked out and the following day we explained ourselves to our uncle. Of course, he was totally fine with what we had done.

We now live in a community where we enjoy the luxury of town water. For most of my life that was not the case. And when you count on wells and pumps to supply water there are often breakdowns. What had become quite normal was that these problems would happen at the most inopportune times. One fall morning, well before sunrise, I awoke to another day only to find a lack of water coming from the taps. As frustrating as it was—after all I couldn't even make a cup of coffee—I suspected this might be a minor issue dealing with a pressure switch.

So early in the morning, while it was still dark, I ventured down to the well. Because the suspected issue was one I had dealt with numerous times before, I did not bring a flashlight. The well had an eight-foot deep "manhole" and at the bottom of this were the pressure switch and other paraphernalia that were required for our water system. I was sure the pressure switch was stuck, so all I would need to do was slip down into the hole and tap the switch. Because I had done this often enough, I thought I would do it without a light. As I was about to enter the darkness of the hole, I heard a noise. Normally that would not deter me but that morning I gave it a second thought and decided I would go get a flashlight.

Heeding my intuition that morning saved me from a significant amount of who knows what. At the bottom of the hole, right where I would have landed with my feet, was a full-grown skunk. I suppose the lid had not been quite right, and as it was scavenging about for breakfast it had fallen into the hole.

That left me with a challenge. I needed to get it out without being sprayed and getting our water supply tainted. If I shot the skunk most of the above would happen. I fetched a thin cable from the barn, fashioned a lasso and managed to get the skunk out with nary a mishap. Although I can now sit back and chuckle about it, I still consider myself fortunate.

In 2011 I received a call from a neighbour lady, and during the course of the conversation she told me she was calling to see whether I was okay. I found the question rather curious. Was I okay? Where do I start? Define okay. I really wondered what she could be referring to. She then told me that she had heard that I had almost drowned. Almost drowned? It took a moment, and then I understood what she was referring to.

That year saw some unprecedented flooding in Western Manitoba. It happened that our home was perched on the edge of the Souris Valley. We had a bird's-eye view of the flooding river. People have asked me, because I was from Wawanesa, whether the flood was impacting us in any way. I often suggested that if our house flooded most of Manitoba would be submerged. I have dreamt of having a lake view property and for three months it was exactly that. It was interesting, intriguing, and, yes, really picturesque. I also understand that what was a scenic view for me was devastating for many folks that lived downstream and around the lakes that the Souris drains into.

When we built that home, we had a difficult time finding a water source. We ended up having to drill a well at the bottom of the valley, not that far from the river. In spring, as the flood began, I could quite easily keep an eye on the well as the trees were without leaves, and so, with binoculars, I monitored the situation. The well was surrounded by water but there never was any danger of it becoming submerged.

Chapter 6 This Happened to Me: Farming with Reckless Abandon

But then things changed, and I decided that I needed to seal our well. In spite of the well being on a ridge and the wellhead being a good three feet above ground level, I felt it was better to be safe than sorry. My wife and I ventured down the hill with our supplies. The plan was simple. I would wade through the water to the well, seal it, and wade back. I did not realize how deep the water was. It turned out it was too deep to wade across. My wife went back to the house to get an air mattress. Perhaps I could use it to swim across. To ensure my safety she also brought back a life jacket. In my mind, I thought that was somewhat unnecessary, but to humour her I donned the life jacket, grabbed the air mattress, and set out.

I did not realize there was a current till my feet could no longer touch ground. Well, there was a current. Instantly, and with some speed, it started taking me towards the river. Not what I had envisioned. I managed to grab a tree and surveyed the situation. My wife offered to go get help. I suggested I could probably make it back but might lose the air mattress. Long story short, I used my legs to push away from the tree and made it back to terra firma. We decided at that point that the well did not need sealing. The water would never get that high. I think that is often referred to as denial. It was the easy way out.

Of course, I never viewed my escapade as being life-threatening. However, thinking back, it could have been a lot more interesting than it was. I imagine a ride down the swollen, frigid Souris River on an air mattress would have been rather unpleasant. It didn't happen. All was well. And to paraphrase Mark Twain, "the reports of my [near] death are greatly exaggerated."

One episode that I do not chuckle about and am loath to talk about because of the stupidity of it, happened a few years prior to the skunk episode. We had built an addition to our barn that included an eight-foot-deep manure storage pit. As we were still in the process of mounting the manure pump, one small section of the pit was open. One morning, as I was loading pigs, one got away on me and ended up falling into the pit which, by now, was half full of manure.

Let me interrupt this story by providing some background. Liquid manure can be lethal because of the gases that are released when the manure is stirred. Not that many years before this, someone I knew had been killed by climbing down into their pit while the manure was being agitated. The deadly effects of the gas are almost instantaneous.

When the pig fell into the pit, I was in a dilemma on how to get it out. As I had finished loading pigs, I decided to haul them away before attempting to rescue the one in the pit. I was convinced that the pig would have succumbed by the time I got back. But there it was, treading manure. Using the same technique as I used with the skunk, I fashioned a lasso out of a small cable. But because manure is not pure liquid, it was difficult to get the lasso around the pig's torso. So, I fetched a ladder, put it into the pit, and proceeded to climb down into the pit. I thought if I held my breath, I should be okay.

The good news is I rescued the pig that day. And perhaps I deserve a medal of bravery for that, but unfortunately the dummy medal I really qualified for would negate anything positive from that experience.

Over the years, I have dealt with countless people who have had life-altering vehicle accidents. I have had the privilege of working with the Manitoba Farmers with Disabilities (MFWD) and their Canadian counterparts. I have heard some horrific stories, stories that made me reflect on my own close calls.

What has really stuck with me is the resilience many of these people showed. Along with that resilience comes a keen sense of humour. At one of the MFWD meetings, everybody laughed when the chairperson called for a vote on a motion, asking people to raise their right hands, hesitated for a second, and then said raising their right hook also counted.

Chapter 6   This Happened to Me: Farming with Reckless Abandon

We laughed when one gentleman, in a wheelchair because of a horrific accident, related his experience of trying to get on the toilet. There wasn't enough room, so he had to go "side saddle." He warned the rest of us that that position can be quite uncomfortable. He told us how he had a real issue when he realized the toilet paper was behind him and he couldn't reach it. Even he found the humour in that.

I had been asked to do a presentation on stress management and, in my preparation, I came across a picture, posted at a gas station, which advertised gas as costing an arm and a leg. I heard laughter when the slide came up. Only after I left the meeting did I realize the implications of that picture and the audience I was speaking to. (Think Friesen, think!)

It was also rewarding talking one on one with many of them. Listening to their stories, some sad, some funny, and hearing them talk about adapting. I chatted with one of them about the irony of a person with a physical impairment feeling free to ask for help and yet people, such as myself, with mental health issues finding it difficult to seek help when we need it. I learned a lot.

After participating in one of these events, I stopped at an indoor driving range, to hit some golf balls. Irony of all ironies, the gentleman hitting balls next to me had only one arm. I was mesmerized by the way he was able to swing a club and make solid contact, shot after shot. You can well imagine, knowing what an avid golfer I am, I had wondered that morning how amputees could farm, never mind enjoy a sport such as golf. It was unfolding right in front of me. What an awesome lesson I learned. Things happen. Things go wrong. But we adapt and move on.

Today I can tell you I am still alive. I have all my body parts. It could have been worse. And often when I meet people who have had life-changing accidents, or I hear of another death involving farm equipment, I just think, there but for the grace of God go I.

Takeaway

Farming can be a very stressful occupation. The World Health Organization has reported that farming is one of the ten most stressful occupations and one of the three most dangerous. Stress that goes unrecognized and is not managed well can cause you to make risky choices. The combination of stress and daily work around powerful machinery in varying and unpredictable situations can lead to accidents.

There are times when stress gives us motivation to accomplish our daily tasks. It provides the adrenaline we need to get jobs done. However, there are times when stress becomes overwhelming, and can have a negative impact on our lives. Stress can become so debilitating that it becomes difficult to function. At times like this, stress can lead to other mental and physical health issues. And when that happens, we jeopardize our personal safety and the safety of others.

It is important to understand the components of stress. Stress is a normal reaction to situations that are perceived to be challenging. However, it is important to understand that it is our reaction to events, not the events themselves, that causes stress. How we react is quite dependent on our resilience and tolerance to stress. Simply speaking, when there is too much stress or long-term stress, it can put us into crisis.

So as much as we cannot control the events of our lives, we can learn to better manage our stress levels. Recognizing the symptoms of stress is not always easy. Stress has a tendency to manifest itself in our physical and mental wellbeing. Perhaps it is an increase in headaches, chest pains, a stiff neck, or sore back. Or we may find that we are more prone to anger, more emotional, experience low self-esteem, or even depression. And as that happens our behaviours change. Our expectations for ourselves and others increase, there may be an increased use of alcohol or drugs, we may have a tendency to isolate ourselves, or we may lose sleep.

Chapter 6 This Happened to Me: Farming with Reckless Abandon

The good news is there are some simple tools that can assist in dealing with stress. Following you will find the six Rs of stress management. (Based on work done by the Manitoba Farm and Rural Stress Line)

1. **RECOGNIZE.** Be aware of when stress becomes overwhelming and has a negative impact on you.
2. **REDUCE.** Do an inventory of your stress and come to an understanding of which stressful items you can control and deal with them. Also learn to accept the things that you cannot control.
3. **RESPOND.** Make sure you treat your body responsibly through healthy nutrition, physical and mental activity, and enough sleep, and take the time to recharge.
4. **RELAX.** Take the time to kick back and enjoy life. Utilize mindfulness techniques such as breathing exercises, yoga, or meditation. And remember to laugh. As they say, laughter is the best medicine.
5. **REACH OUT.** Identify your support system. Verbalizing your thoughts and feelings can be helpful. You will find it normalizes and validates the feelings you are experiencing.
6. **RESOURCES.** Remember that there are resources available. Sometimes the nearest and best resource is a family member or friend to talk to. Other times it may be important to seek professional help.

It is not the experiences of today that create the most stress. Rather it is a reflection of the past or dread for tomorrow that tends to create an overwhelming sense of stress. Meeting challenges one at a time is a good approach to stress management. By focusing on today you may be surprised at the renewed energy you have for the day and for an enhanced life for tomorrow. It may save your life.

Chapter 7
A Mennonite: To Be or Not to Be

I enter the church and sit in a row halfway up the sanctuary. Outside darkness has fallen, but here I am again. It's a revival service, so I am nervous and apprehensive. My parents would have suggested it was conviction, that feeling of already being sentenced as a sinner, and who was I to argue? Then one of my worst fears happens. An older fellow with a seizure disorder sits down beside me. It frightens me. I have seen him have a seizure, and it is scary. As the service begins, the preacher asks people if they would want to share a testimony. In my mind I am convinced that if I don't get up and say something, surely God will make that man have a seizure. Finally with shaking knees and a quivering voice, I get up and blurt out something. He did not have a seizure that evening.

Truth be told I am actually a Mexican Mennonite. Okay, that may be an overstatement, but I do hold a Mexican birth certificate. It's written entirely in Spanish, so I have no clue what it says. My parents moved to Mexico as missionaries in 1959. I have often wondered but never did ask, not sure I really want to know, but when they made the move, my mother was four months

Chapter 7   A Mennonite: To Be or Not to Be

pregnant. Seems to me there was some poor planning involved or perhaps something unexpected happened. Regardless, a week before Christmas I entered the world. Perhaps it was the nine months in the womb or my journey through the birth canal, but something was not right with my mother, so five months after my birth my parents had to move back to Canada due to my mother's health issues.

I grew up in a home that can only be described as a fundamental Mennonite home. Even as I write this, I find myself being somewhat confused as to what that really means. I suppose I could spend some time laying out who left which church in which country because of beliefs that seemed to be somewhat fluid, always changing, as certain people would find different ways of interpreting scriptures. Suffice it to say, that would take considerable time and do nothing for the intent and purpose of my story.

In simple terms, the faith of my parents could be categorized under the umbrella of *klein gemeinde*, meaning "small church." The core basis of that was to live righteously, be part of and support the church, help those in need and don't go to war. And although that might have been the basis, and it sounds simple enough, someone was constantly changing rules that came with being followers of that faith. And when someone felt that the rules of the church were becoming too liberal or to conservative, new churches would start up.

There is a story told of a Mennonite, let's call him Jac, who was shipwrecked on an island. After many years he was able to flag down a passing ship. When the captain and crew of the ship came ashore, Jac offered to give them a tour of his island. Jac showed them a quaint little house he had built for himself. He showed them a barn where he had been able to keep some animals. Finally, he showed them the church he had built and worshipped in. The captain expressed his admiration for what Jac had accomplished. But then he pointed to another building, which Jac had not shown them, and asked what that was. Jac answered by saying that was the church he used to belong to.

We were taught to be "in the world, but not of the world." Having a TV, a Christmas tree, being involved in community events, having fancy cars, and a host of other things, were not permitted. I grew up in an era in which men and women would sit on separate sides in church. Women wore head coverings, and, in some cases, men still needed to have beards. So which church or denomination you adhered to dictated what you could or could not do.

I still remember when my father wanted to start wearing a tie for preaching. That involved church patriarchs paying a visit to discuss it and pray about it. When my father wanted to buy a new car, it had to be ordered from the factory because it was standard by now that cars came with radios and that was a no-no. When the only car that was available had a radio, it caused my parents great consternation.

And to add to this confusion, my father came from a more conservative community and family than my mother, so how we dressed and how we acted changed depending which family we were getting together with. For example, one Christmas when we had relatives over, the more liberal types, we could put tinsel on a fern. And having a radio in your car was perfectly fine for one family but certainly not the other one.

In 1966 my parents were part of a group that moved to another community. They were part of a large congregation in southeastern Manitoba, a congregation that felt it important to move into various areas to evangelize, to be a shining light, to fulfill, as they saw it, a calling from God.

The move took place during my first-grade year. As is often the case with well-laid plans, the process of selling and relocating didn't proceed without its share of challenges. My parents had successfully sold their farm located near Blumenort in southeastern

Chapter 7 A Mennonite: To Be or Not to Be

Manitoba. However, they had to vacate the premises before their new house near Wawanesa, in western Manitoba, was fully prepared, which presented a bit of a conundrum. What they ended up doing was temporarily moving into a house trailer situated on my aunt's property in Landmark. They resided there for about a month before ultimately moving to their new home in November.

Imagine, as a six-year-old, I embarked on an educational journey that took me through three different schools in a single year. During the first month of that school year, I walked a mile to reach my school. That seems rather hard to fathom today. The second month, at the second school, brought a change, as I was fortunate enough to catch a ride with my aunt, who was coincidentally also my teacher. And when we moved to Wawanesa, my mode of transportation shifted again, this time by bus. Such a diverse array of schools and transportation methods in my early years. And people wonder why I need therapy.

The people in the community of Wawanesa were rather apprehensive as this group of families moved in. What was strange to them was that ten families purchased the land that was formerly farmed by two brothers. They were convinced that these families would become a social burden on the community. However, being Mennonite meant that these families were quite attuned to livestock production and so in each yard barns were constructed, for chickens, turkeys or hogs.

The cultural differences in the communities were significant. Moving from a primarily Mennonite community to an English community provided for some interesting adaptations. We did not speak English at home, rather our parents wanted us to be fluent in both low German and high German. They knew that we would learn English when we went to school. I can only assume that the cultural differences were just as confusing to the English kids as they were to us.

My upbringing in a strict Mennonite household presented its own set of challenges. Compounding the stress was the fact that my father served as our church's pastor. Apart from attending school and assisting with farm duties, the church played a central role in my life. I often suggest, albeit in a lighthearted manner, that if the church lights were on, you could bet I was there.

The role of a pastor's son bore its unique burdens, involving a distinct set of expectations. Not only was I part of a small minority within the school, but I was also a minority within the church community, courtesy of my status as a preacher's kid. This less than distinctive position seemed to provide endless amusement for many.

In the Wawanesa school, dancing was part of the curriculum and certainly formed part of any concerts put on by the school. Shortly after becoming part of the community, my father and another church patriarch attended a square dance put on by my grade-two class. The sole purpose of the visit was to tell the school administration that Mennonite kids should not be required to participate. And, God forbid, in grade seven when it was time for sex education, I was not allowed to participate and had to leave the classroom. Not sure what the reason was for that, it just simply meant I was self-taught. And that was before the days of Google. Enough said.

My parents had a strong belief and did their utmost to ensure that their kids would remain true to that faith. We were ruled by guilt and manipulation with guilt. Whenever we strayed, the grip of discipline was swift and unyielding. For all intents and purposes, their main mission was to keep us from going to hell. That meant a host of different rules we had to follow. Some made sense, others not so much. I can't help but wonder if Jesus had more fun growing up than I did.

In retrospect, that concept of Christianity created significant inner turmoil for me. As much as I tried, as much as I would

Chapter 7 A Mennonite: To Be or Not to Be

confess to everything that I thought might be a sin, the assurance that I was "saved" was elusive. It just never seemed to be enough.

Going to church was not just a Sunday morning event. There were always numerous other church functions happening, including programs, missionaries reporting on their work, communion, church membership meetings, and, of course, the bi-annual deeper life meetings. The deeper life services, once called revival meetings, were held to revitalize the church community and to bring lost souls to redemption. They normally would involve altar calls as well, which provided the opportunity for folks to publicly show their desire to follow the Christian faith.

Some I have shared this story with get a confused look on their face when I mention "altar call." Let me explain. Altar calls happened quite frequently in churches, particularly at revival meetings. Normally these services were held because there were those that slipped in their Christianity and needed to rededicate themselves. As well there were those that had never been "born again," and so the pressure was on to bring those lost souls to Jesus. Often, if not always, the visiting ministers would preach fire and brimstone. If nothing else, the intent was to scare people to redemption. So at the end of each service there would be an altar call. The song of choice for this was "Just As I Am." And as the song was sung, people were invited to go forward to receive salvation. Sometimes the song was sung more than once, depending on the response. To this day, that song sends shivers down my back as I feel my mother prodding me, figuratively speaking, to go forward.

As young adults, two of my friends and I would sometimes cynically practice these altar calls. We would take turns being song leader or preacher. I recall one day we took our girlfriends to the beach. The three of us sat in the front seat of the car—this was before bucket seats—spending half an hour playing the game. We took turns singing "Just As I Am" and role-playing as preachers, inviting an imaginary group of people to come forward to receive salvation.

A few years later, shortly after we moved back to the farm, my wife and I became the youth leaders in our church. As it happens the church held a week of services. Thursday night, the focus was on youth, and so as youth leader, I led the service, which included leading the singing. At the end of the service, I had picked a song to sing, but as I was announcing the page number to the congregation the preacher stepped up and asked us to sing "Just As I Am."

Who was I to argue? After all, I had practiced this, but inwardly I shuddered. As I stood there, I couldn't help but wonder, what if my friends could see me now? Inwardly I was laughing but needed to remain serious. From my vantage point I noticed my wife quickly leaving her pew, not to come forward but rather to step out of the sanctuary. She just could not keep herself from laughing about the irony of the situation I found myself in.

As much as the basis of the Mennonite faith created confusion, one of the true aspects of my parents' faith was caring for and about others. And community certainly became part of who my parents were. Moving from a primarily Mennonite community to a completely non-Mennonite community must have been a cultural shock for them. As they grew into this new reality, their approach changed as well. Furthermore, when they left their pastoral position and began a prison ministry, their community expanded even more as they dealt with, talked to, and cared for the less fortunate.

Early in our new life in Wawanesa, they felt it important to connect with the teachers from school. In an effort to get to know them better, they would invite two or three at a time to come to our house for coffee and a visit. Not sure about you, but I lived in mortal fear of my teachers. So imagine the terror I felt when I was in grade four and saw my teacher and principal walking through our door. And yet, as I found out later in life, that invitation left a lasting impression on the teachers.

The last time I attended a church the minister got up and the very first sentence out of his mouth was "the entire premise of the

Chapter 7   A Mennonite: To Be or Not to Be

gospel is community". That, quite frankly, was the most profound statement I had ever heard from a preacher. I leaned over and told my wife that he could have stopped right there. Enough said, let's go home. If all of us would take that to heart, if we would all love our neighbors as we love ourselves, the world would be a much better place.

I have come to the understanding that many of the things I was taught at home and in church seem to be diametrically opposed to what I believe today. So perhaps I did not leave the Mennonite church, but rather it left me.

If that's the case, why would I still identify as a Mennonite? Quite frankly it's difficult not to with my last name. Friesen is a common Mennonite name. Based on 2014 numbers, one in 166,075 people or about 48,000 people in the world, bear the name Friesen. At one point in time, my lineage of Friesen was known as Von Riesen. To simplify things, they changed it to Friesen. Rather unfortunate, I think, as Von Riesen has a certain regal ring to it. Perhaps I should change back. Say it out loud: Geraldo Von Riesen. I like it!

I would be remiss in not talking about Mennonite food. Growing up, the meals in our house were quite basic. In retrospect, my mother wasn't particularly adventurous in her meal prep. I was raised on *shmaunt fat, shinke fleish, keilke, verenika*, and *forma vorscht*, (cream gravy, ham, egg noodles, perogies and farmer sausage). She did, on occasion, cook liver. That did not go over well with us kids. It was only when we could show her, in our newly purchased *World Book Encyclopedia*, what the function of the liver is, that she quit that.

On one of my trips to Japan, I sat with a Japanese gentleman who had spent a month in Manitoba as a chaperone for a student exchange. I asked about his experiences, particularly as it concerned adjusting to Canadian food. He told me how he had lived with a Mennonite family near Steinbach. He suggested that most of the food had been quite good, however, he had really struggled with egg noodles (kielke). He said that boiled egg noodles had a disgusting odor. I almost choked on my shark fin soup! Really? Kielke has always been one of my favorites and still is. However, the next time I ate those I did the sniff test and realized he was right. They do really stink. I still like them.

And we shouldn't forget about the language. As mentioned previously, my parents thought it important that we learn high German. That became our "home" language till I was fifteen years old. Mixed in with that was low German, which I also became fluent in before learning the English language. Seeing as my wife was also raised in a Mennonite home, we can and do, at times, speak low German. And here is the irony of the low German dialect. My roots are from the east side of the Red River. My wife was raised on the west side. And although the communities are only an hour apart, the pronunciation of many words is different. Both being able to speak the language was quite handy when we wanted to say something that we didn't want our kids to understand. That even works now with our grandkids, and the looks they give us when we speak German is priceless.

Takeaway

In a conversation with a farmer several years ago, he related how financial stress and relational issues had caused him significant distress. He told me how the simple act of changing clothes when entering the barn seemed to be a major chore. I strongly suggested he needed to go seek help from a professional. He then asked me whether seeing his pastor wouldn't be just as helpful. I responded by asking him if he would go see his pastor if he broke his leg.

As I left his farm that day, I was troubled by the answer I had given him. Perhaps I had been too blunt with my response. I also wondered if he felt less stigma about seeing his pastor instead of a mental health professional. In my mind I was strongly of

Chapter 7 A Mennonite: To Be or Not to Be

the opinion that a mental health injury is no different than a physical injury. And for healing, it is important to find the right medical help.

In my next visit with that farmer, we talked further about that previous conversation. He was open about the importance of his faith in dealing with challenges that he faced. He suggested that seeking pastoral help worked in deepening his faith, finding a renewed connection to a higher being and with that be better at coping with all his stress.

In other conversations, I have also heard how seeking help from spiritual leaders deepened the issues that these people were dealing with. In one situation, a person sought help from their pastor and ended up being berated for his poor mental health. He was told that he wasn't working hard enough. In another case, a sexual abuse survivor was told to forgive and forget, that there was a lack of understanding why sexual abuse happened, and so there was nothing else they could suggest.

I think it is important to distinguish between religion and spirituality. Religion, in essence, consists of a set of organized beliefs and practices, and often those beliefs are held with certainty and not questioned. And, as I experienced, this can hinder the development of building spirituality and mental wellness.

Spirituality, on the other hand, is something practiced by individuals to bring about peace and purpose. It's a belief that there is something greater than us, something beyond what we feel as humans. Practicing spirituality comes in various forms. It can include meditation, going for walks, spending time in nature, journaling, and others. And before you assume I am excluding church from the equation, spirituality may indeed encompass participation in a spiritual community or organized religion.

Most of what is listed above as being part of spirituality are mainstays of any information that speaks to coping mechanisms. They provide meaning and purpose. They enhance connection and the feeling of belonging. They help in building resilience. They increase awareness and make space to practice compassion, both for yourself and for others.

Spirituality is not a stand-alone remedy for coping and dealing with mental illness. Rather its another tool that can be used. We should never limit ourselves. Often it's a combination of multiple tricks that will help the most. The important message in this is that there are many different tools and resources available to help us find ways to cope with and improve our mental health. It is up to us to find those resources and use them.

And ultimately there may be times when those resources may not be enough. We must also make sure that we reach out when that is needed. If that is a spiritual leader and that works for you, great. If it doesn't work, then find another professional to talk to. There is hope and there is relief.

Chapter 8
When Columbus Sailed the Ocean Blue: Discovering the Giant Within

I awake from a restless sleep hoping that it will be morning. All I want is to fly home and find sanctuary in my hog barn. I am in Montreal, meeting with people I do not know about business that is completely foreign to me, representing people who, for some strange reason, have confidence in me. My anxiety overwhelms me. How can I ever fulfill my duties as the leader of the organization I am representing. How can I possibly face people back home knowing how much I really don't know.

Over the course of the first eight years of farming, our farm had progressed to the point where other interests were creeping in. A lot of work had gone into developing the hog operation and expanding the turkey operation. As eager participants in our respective commodities, my brother and I attended a lot of different meetings. Whether annual meetings, district meetings, or information meetings, we tried to get to them all.

In the early '90s, while attending a hog producer meeting, I was elected to a leadership role with Manitoba Pork Est., an organization that represented all hog farmers in the province, marketed all the hogs produced in Manitoba, and spent time and energy in the promotion of the industry and the products we produced.

I found it difficult to participate. I had very little confidence in what I had to say, never sure whether it was relevant or pertinent. This made for many nervous moments when I would try to say something but found it difficult to articulate because I was so unsure of myself. My voice would quiver, and I would literally choke on words.

When I attended my first board meeting, all decked out in a suit and tie, I felt great pride when I was informed that I was being appointed to be Manitoba Pork's representative on the executive of the Keystone Agricultural Producers, Manitoba's general farm organization. The pride I felt was short lived as I realized that come the next annual meeting I would have to get up in front of producers and industry representatives to give my report. The low self-esteem and lack of confidence I had lived with really hit home, to the point where I considered quitting the board just to relieve the pressure.

As with all other things in my life, the learning curve was steep. There were numerous hot button issues that were being dealt with at the time. And perhaps no more or no less than previously or what would be dealt with in the future. Aside from ongoing marketing issues, such as pricing, grading, and others, there were grain transportation changes, constant discussions on safety nets, environmental concerns were coming to the forefront, and animal welfare concerns were on the rise. Along with regular meetings, we would meet with government, packers, producers, and other hog jurisdictions. Everything I was learning about in short order had never had any importance in my life previously. They probably should have, because all those issues were directly impacting my own farm.

Along with the many issues that the board dealt with, there were other opportunities to participate in. It involved travel to

Chapter 8   When Columbus Sailed the Ocean Blue

other parts of the world. Because a large percentage of the pork produced in Manitoba was exported, the government would often put together trade missions to visit our customers. That would mean trips to countries such as Japan, Taiwan, and South Korea. Or due to changing environmental rules, we would visit England, Holland, Denmark, and Belgium, countries that were front runners in adapting to changing regulations on environmental stewardship. We would visit other jurisdictions in Canada and the United States, to tour packing plants and meet with our customers and other producer groups.

I visited farms in many of the places I travelled to. I experienced cultures far removed from my own. I stepped far beyond my own comfort zone. In essence my involvement allowed me to experience agriculture around the world.

Initially it felt good being elected. It gave my self-esteem a boost. It gave me a sense of importance. But often, late at night, sitting in another hotel room, the reality of the situation would hit. I had been thrust from the obscure security of my farm into the bigger world of agricultural politics. Furthermore, that morphed into meetings, trade shows, and trade missions nationally and internationally. It reminded me of Christopher Columbus. It has sometimes been said that when he set sail, he had no idea where he was going, he didn't know how to get there, and when he did get there, he had no idea where he was.

I felt lost in this new world. I was not sure how I ended up there. And I certainly did not have the confidence to know what I was supposed to do there. That early morning in Montreal, as I was pondering my situation, I discovered how alcohol could give me relief from the anxiety I was feeling. I found it gave me the courage to do what I didn't think I could. It helped breach the chasm between my lack of confidence and the courage and strength I needed to carry out the duties that I had been elected to do. (More on this in Chapter 13.)

When I became chairman in 1996, the industry was in flux. Since 1965 all producers had been legislated to market their hogs through the Manitoba Hog Producers Marketing Commission, often referred to as single desk selling, which later became Manitoba Pork Est. In 1995 the provincial government began the process of eliminating that legislation. In their opinion, single desk selling was an impediment for the industry to grow. And in their estimation, based on various factors, they saw an opportunity for the industry to significantly increase production and boost the provincial economy.

The concept of open marketing, or producer choice, was a frightening concept to many. For some of the older producers, the memory of what had been before single desk selling was still raw. It was strongly felt that removing single desk selling would create chaos in the marketplace; the very reason single desk selling had been initiated in the first place. Many suggested that the change to an open marketing system would spell the demise of the family farm. The tension between producers and the government was intense. So instead of leading discussions on the policies and operations of the organization, I jumped into that cauldron of high emotion.

That change in marketing meant numerous meetings with the minister of agriculture. Along with the government's insistence that the legislation would change, the minister also took a position on some other issues that were quite frustrating for us.

I sometimes suggest that what I lack in knowledge, I make up for with passion, a trait not always well received. My tendency is to say little, until I shouldn't say anything, and then I say too much. And so, on occasion, I would let loose with a verbal barrage. Perhaps I am passive aggressive. Whatever the case, perhaps because of weariness or frustration, there are times when nothing can hold me back.

Chapter 8   When Columbus Sailed the Ocean Blue

I will never forget the day we walked into the minister's office and before he had a chance to say much, I went into an impassioned speech about our position on an issue that had been discussed on numerous occasions. He sat quietly and listened and when I was finished, he calmly looked at me and said that he was backing down from his position and we could carry on as we saw fit. Obviously that decision had been made prior to the meeting, and if I had given him a chance, he would have given us the answer before I went into my tirade. When we shook hands that day before we left, we were both able to chuckle about the way the meeting had gone.

That was not the only time I became passionate as we worked through the process. One day, while being somewhat busy on the farm, I needed to deal with an issue with the deputy minister. I tried calling him, but he did not answer, so I left him a message. That was one of those times when I wished I could have pulled the message off his phone before he had a chance to listen to it. I did not realize how passionate I had become till my brother, who had walked up behind me during the diatribe, suggested that he had never heard anyone talk to a bureaucrat like that before. After some reflection, I called back. Again, he did not answer, so I left him another message. I said I was sorry with the first message I had left him. I explained that I felt strongly about the point I was trying to make but that the delivery had been wrong. Again, something we were able to chuckle about later.

On another occasion, I was talking on the phone with another bureaucrat. The discussion went on for quite some time and both of us were rather passionate about the subject at hand. At the end of our conversation, he said that he was going to go to a driving range that night and was going to pretend my face was on every ball. When I hung up from that call I went to my wife, who had clearly heard my side of the conversation, and suggested that I sure would have liked to have told the guy to f**k off. She turned to me and said, with a smile, that it sounded like I had. All these years later, that gentleman and I will reminisce about our conversations over a cup of coffee and share a laugh.

As the industry evolved, my role changed as well. I became president of the Manitoba Pork Marketing Co-op, an organization that provided services for those producers who still embraced collective marketing. The manager of the newly formed coop and I had become friends.

He was the sales manager when I first became involved with Manitoba Pork Est. Together we had been tasked to visit sow buyers in the US. I knew little about sows, even less about markets, and really was not sure what I could contribute. Along with that, I did not really know the sales manager. I wasn't sure whether I was accompanying him or whether he was accompanying me. I clearly was not ready for taking leadership. However, that trip proved to be the beginning of a long and lasting friendship. As we travelled through South Dakota and Iowa, we really started to get to know each other, not realizing at the time how important that friendship would become, both professionally and personally.

First and foremost, we were trying to build a marketing organization that hog producers would embrace. Along with that, our organization became involved in hog production through a company called Dynamic Pork. The hog industry was in constant turmoil and prices could best be described as a roller coaster. Trade actions were creating uncertainties. That meant that the industry and our producers were not faring well. It involved numerous and constant conversations between the two of us.

All that took a toll on our personal lives as well. And over the years, as I struggled with my mental health and he faced some significant health challenges, we would literally use each other's shoulder to cry on. As he once said, we seemed to have the ability to sense when one of us was nearing an abyss, and when that happened, the other would reach out and provide support.

Chapter 8 When Columbus Sailed the Ocean Blue

My involvement in agricultural politics provided me with some important life lessons. First of all, I was searching for the source of my power but was clearly looking in all the wrong places. As much as I came to understand that I had more power within than I was giving myself credit for, I came to the realization that much of my power came from without. The very confidence that others were showing in me was providing the encouragement and power to do what I needed to do. Only after that realization could I effectively draw strength from other people, to accomplish far greater things than I had ever thought possible.

I learned that I did not need to change who I was or try to be someone I wasn't. I was a much better leader when I became authentic and realized my strengths but also my weaknesses. That meant that I didn't have to carry the burden alone. I always had the good fortune of working with fellow producers, board directors, and staff, towards common goals. That helped me be the leader I never knew I could be.

In retrospect, much of what I learned from my experiences through those years was integral to the work I moved into as my own farm wound down. I suppose it is a situation we often experience. We go through struggles, we wish some things had never happened, but after the fact, we often look back and understand that certain experiences were not enjoyable, but in the bigger picture of life, they were helpful in shaping and molding who we became.

Takeaway

Often when folks find themselves in situations that are new to them, they will find the power within to manage that situation. They seem to have the confidence, poise, and self-esteem to do what needs to be done. Other times, people seem to get lost in their insecurities. When challenges arise or new opportunities come, they shy away from them. They don't feel they have the ability and confidence to deal with them.

I have a friend who has been teaching high school and university students for many years. In a conversation, I asked him what made him successful as a teacher. He told me that he *didn't* teach. He went on to explain that his students had the knowledge within and what he was doing was helping them find it.

That resonated with me. I drew a comparison to my perceived incapabilities when I became a leader. Through a learning process, I came to understand that I did have the abilities. And the reason I was able to learn that was due to the people who put me there. They were the ones that recognized the potential. I was surrounded by people who helped me strive to do better. When I stumbled or faltered, they understood and helped me be better. And with their guidance and support, I was able to be the most I could be. The power from without helped me find the power from within.

Those resources, particularly those folks who saw the potential, helped me discover that giant within. Columbus did not discover a brand-new world on his own. He had help from others, and he took advantage of those resources to accomplish his discovery.

We all need to recognize that we have a giant within us. What's important to understand is that the people we surround ourselves with will help in discovering the giant. So often we miss what others see in us. Or we discount it, not believing what others see. Or in my case, even thinking I didn't deserve it.

Through believing in yourself, by taking control of your life and through the support of others, you can discover the giant within. And as you do, you will find the strength, courage, and ability to accomplish things never before imagined.

Chapter 9
Can We All Just Get Along? Turning Judgement to Curiosity

I am sitting across the table from a couple facing some significant and frustrating financial issues on their farm. Despite their relentless efforts, their struggles have yielded nothing but frustration. I can feel their agitation as their very existence, their way of life, is being threatened. As much as they have tried, nothing has worked. And now the creditors are poised to take further action. As I start explaining that the purpose of us being there is to help them, the gentleman across the table suddenly jumps to his feet, his eyes filled with fury, and starts coming across the table at me.

In the fall of 1999, I got a call that changed my life. The minister of agriculture phoned and asked whether I would consider an appointment to the Manitoba Farm Mediation Board. At first blush, I felt honoured for having been asked but also hesitant about accepting the appointment. She explained that she was seeking to appoint people who had expertise in the various commodities produced in our province. She felt that with my experience in hog production and the added experience of my involvement in

Manitoba Pork, I would be a good fit. I told her that I would need to think about that.

The request came when our farm was still experiencing the lingering effects of the hog price crash of 1998. We were on the brink of insolvency. How could I possibly fulfill my duties on the mediation board? When I phoned the minister's assistant the following day, I shared with her my apprehension, telling her that I might well be a candidate for the board's services in the near future. She then informed me that my name had already been put forward to cabinet for approval. With significant trepidation, I decided to accept the role.

Again, I had to go through a significant learning experience. I did not know what my role would be. All I knew, or assumed, was when farmers were involved with the mediation board, it meant that they were in financial trouble.

I learned quickly enough that the farm mediation legislation came about as the result of high interest rates in the late '70s and early '80s. When the rates peaked at 20 percent, many farmers were faced with insurmountable debt issues. So the government stepped in and provided a safety net for farmers. With the help of a third party, farmers were given a chance to negotiate terms and conditions that would see them keep farming.

My curiosity grew as I approached my first board meeting in the spring of 2000. What I quickly learned is that I would be actively involved in farm debt files. I would meet with farmers and creditors to establish recovery plans. And, in worst case scenarios, those discussions could well involve the wind down of operations that were in too deep to recover. Without any formal training, I became a mediator.

I quickly came to understand a fundamental characteristic about myself. For the previous ten years I had been involved in scenarios that demanded negotiating skills. I had often felt that I

Chapter 9 Can We All Just Get Along? Turning Judgement to Curiosity

was not an effective negotiator. When I began mediating, I came to the realization that I had intuitively been using mediation skills.

Instead of taking a position and passionately and adamantly sticking to it, I would be interested in hearing both sides of the story. I was interested in hearing why packers couldn't pay more for hogs. I really wanted to know why the government was intent on removing single desk selling. I tried to understand why environmental rules had to change. And after hearing both sides of the issues, I would try to figure out how an equitable agreement could be reached.

Furthermore, when I was chairman of Manitoba Pork and then president of Manitoba Pork Marketing, I always tried to achieve consensus around the board table. It bothered me when an issue went to a vote and there were those that would vote against something. And when that happened, I needed to understand why. Sometimes it made sense, and I would be okay with it. Other times I became frustrated when I realized that there had not been enough discussion to provide better understanding.

Due to that self-reflection, I felt I had found a new career path, something I could pursue as my interest in the farm grew less. To improve my skills, I decided to learn more about conflict and conflict management. I looked at different training opportunities and so began my post-secondary education.

I enrolled in an introductory conflict resolution course at the University of Winnipeg. I chuckled the day I went in to meet with a student advisor. He thought I was there for one of my kids and was surprised when he found out I was going to be a student. I did not chuckle so much the first night I walked into the classroom. It was somewhat daunting to see a bunch of students, the same age as my kids, in the classroom.

However, I sat down, and thus began a journey of discovery and learning. I might have been the oldest student in the class, but what I found—and the professor acknowledged—is that because of my life experiences it was much easier to understand the theories and concepts I was learning. I was able to apply them to real life situations, which made them easier to understand.

Through some university courses and further training with a nonprofit organization involved in mediation training in my area, I became a certified mediator. As much as conflict management seemed to be part of my nature, I clearly had a lot to learn.

One of the more significant concepts I would need to learn was that, as a mediator, I needed to be neutral. Initially that was challenging for me, but as I grew into the role it became easier. I learned quickly that there are at least two sides to every story and sometimes three or four.

I found that my training in conflict management played a role in my personal life as well. My approach to relationships changed as I learned conflict management techniques. In one assignment I had to complete for a university course, I was asked to interview someone that would have noticed this change. I was always curious whether my approach to dealing with my kids might have changed.

Their response, while not surprising, did fill me with sadness but encouragement as well. They concurred that for most of their lives I would get quite agitated when dealing with conflict. I would try to resolve situations by raising my voice. That obviously did nothing to calm the situation. Then when I started my training, they noticed my response to conflict changing. They found I was a lot calmer and much more open to hearing both sides of the conflict, reframing and paraphrasing, and then discussing the issue until a consensus was reached.

To a point, that was appreciated. One evening my daughter asked about using a car. She asked her mother who told her to ask her father. She approached me with the question but was quick to suggest we not talk about it. Just a simple yes or no. However, when my answer was no, she was quite ready to talk about it.

Chapter 9   Can We All Just Get Along? Turning Judgement to Curiosity

My wife will sometimes suggest that I start fights just to practice my mediation skills. But ultimately, she too has recognized how my conflict management training has changed my approach to many situations. Having said that, she does remain concerned about the equanimity piece of my life. Often when we are driving, and I am expressing my frustrations about other drivers, she will comment about how she can't believe I am a mediator. I would like to think it's a work in progress.

In 2003 another opportunity came about. The Federal Government was looking for mediators for their own farm debt legislation. As you can well imagine, the criteria to meet the qualifications for a federal contract were significant and onerous. It just did not seem that I would qualify, so I left it. Then two days before the Request for Proposals was due, I decided I had nothing to lose. And as it turns out, my application was accepted.

As I delved deeper into the field of farm debt mediation, I started considering opportunities to broaden my professional horizons. With the decision made in 2005 to sell our farm, it became evident that this was the ideal moment to embark on a new venture. Consequently, in 2006, I started my own conflict management practice called Signature Mediation.

In 2011, totally by accident, I came across an email asking for mediators. The Manitoba Public Insurance Corporation had started a pilot project. The work would involve mediating between the corporation and claimants who had been hurt in motor vehicle accidents but were not satisfied with the benefits they were receiving. I sent a letter of interest along with my résumé and was accepted to the roster of mediators for the Automobile Injury Mediation Office.

People who are facing financial stress, the loss of a dream, or have had life changing accidents, often deal with emotions that are foreign to them. They react in various ways. The gentleman I mentioned at the outset was overcome with frustration with his farm financial struggles. The frustration was so great he was not able to recognize, at first, that we were there to assist. As we chatted further that day, that recognition set in. Over the course of the following years, he and I chatted frequently. I became a trusted friend; one he could turn to as the challenges of farming would overwhelm him.

In another situation, my client sat across from me, using language best not repeated here. He apologized for the language, but I assured him I was quite familiar with it, after all I am an avid golfer. I listened as he vented. I tried to normalize and validate his feelings. And then he looked at me and suggested I had no idea what he was talking about. I stopped him, and let him know, without too many gory details, about my own journey, about the challenges I had faced. He gave me a startled look and said, "you really know what I am talking about." A connection was made.

In many of the situations I deal with, those connections become an integral part of the process. My clients often feel lost in trying to navigate the issues they are dealing with. In many cases, there is a significant power imbalance. The clients feel small when they face creditors or insurance companies. So the process needs someone to bring a balance to the discussion. And often that means that I need to help in building understanding, do some reality checking, and provide the ability to explore options. To do that requires connection.

To be meaningfully connected requires an emotional connection. That is particularly true when dealing with folks in family mediation, for example. These types of conflict often require unpacking significant history in relationships and at times deal with "ugly" stuff. Being connected, showing empathy and trying to remain impartial can be difficult. I also found that when I avoided making an emotional connection, people sensed that and were not as open to sharing in an honest and open way.

Chapter 9   Can We All Just Get Along? Turning Judgement to Curiosity

That left me with a real conundrum. Too much connection, or empathy, left me exposed to becoming partial to one side or the other. Not enough connection led to unresolved issues. Furthermore, I have also come to an understanding that I must be aware of my own emotional wellbeing when I mediate. When dealing with individuals in crisis, that emotional connection can be emotionally draining, leaving me ineffective as a mediator and negatively impacting my own mental health.

In my struggles with self-doubt, I often question my abilities to be a mediator. I leave situations never knowing if I helped or if, in fact, I made things worse. But in private moments, I do pride myself in having the ability to connect. And maybe, just maybe, I can look at my own experiences and understand that they do help me in my work.

On occasion, I am asked to present to a university class for some colleagues. For the most part I am asked to talk about farm debt legislation in Manitoba. It's a subject that tends to be rather tedious and boring. Normally a colleague is in the room to introduce me and then ask the required questions to make it appear that someone was listening.

Just recently, as I made my way to the university, I was somewhat concerned. Neither one of my colleagues would be there to make the introduction, so I was on my own. I would need to find the classroom and introduce myself without their help. In addition, I had a flight to catch right after the class, so I found myself not entirely engaged in the task at hand.

I found the right room by asking a student, walked in, sat on a chair in the front of the room and assessed the situation. The classroom was quite large and the dozen or so students were spread out in the room. Most of them looked less enthused than I felt.

When the class started, I introduced myself, told them about the work I do, and then told the students they had an option. They could either listen to me present on farm debt legislation, something rather boring, or they could ask questions about my work, which could create a conversation. The questions came quick and turned into an interesting hour, at least for me. Although with ten minutes left, one of the students suggested I could leave early to ensure I caught my flight. Clearly, he was not enjoying it as much as me.

One of the first questions that was asked was what had been one of the most interesting farm files I had dealt with. I had to do some quick thinking and began telling stories about a couple of files that came to mind. As it turned out, I thought about that more as I waited for my flight at the airport and realized which file had turned out to be the most interesting, the most fun and heartbreaking all at the same time, and probably the most successful end result I have seen.

I played a number of different roles in this file. I was a farm debt mediator, a family mediator, assisted in the execution of a will, chair of an advisory board, a surrogate father, and ultimately a friend. Here is their story as I remember it.

I met Jim and his father Jack (not their real names) in March of 2008 at a farm debt mediation meeting. I will never forget that day, sitting in the lobby of the hotel and Jack walking up to me and asking a question about some event in the United States and the impact it would have on global events. Something, quite frankly, I had never thought of. Over the years I would get to know Jack a lot better and come to understand what a deep thinker he was.

Jim and Jack farmed in Southern Manitoba. Jim's mom and dad had separated when he was four, so he spent significant time farming with his dad. His dad sometimes told me he had toilet trained Jim on the axle of the auger. Based on that alone, it is easy to imagine Jim's active participation on the farm, starting at an early age. It also becomes quite easy to imagine the activities on the farm with Jim operating equipment and driving trucks when

Chapter 9   Can We All Just Get Along? Turning Judgement to Curiosity

hitting the gas and looking out of the windshield was a challenge, but he somehow managed even that.

Jim regaled me with stories of various escapades whether it was driving his muscle car, dirt bikes, or a host of other vehicles, some roadworthy, others not so much. I suspect most of us could share stories of our younger years, but at some point, a certain maturity kicks in. He has always remained young at heart and, at times, pays the price for wanting to get from point A to point B as quickly as possible. So if he showed up with his arm in a sling, we would not waste time on formalities or sympathy. Rather it was just him telling me about his latest escapades, usually with a smile on his face.

He would not hesitate to try something new. In the last year or two, he took up motocross racing. Normally reserved for a younger crowd, he seemed to fit right in. This winter he found a girlfriend who liked cross-country skiing. On his first go, she had forgotten to mention that cross-country skis are significantly different than downhill skis. As he came to the crest of a hill, he did what he does best. Point the skis downhill and hope for the best. The result—a tangled mess of skis, limbs, and trees. When I met him the following day, he had a sheepish grin on his face. When he explained the story behind his bruised face, I couldn't help myself. I laughed and so did he.

Shortly after that original farm debt meeting, Jim contacted me to enquire whether I could work with him and his dad on relational issues. The farm business was experiencing financial challenges and the relationship between dad and son was also deteriorating. It was a classic story of generational differences combined with financial challenges and a significant lack of communication.

I met with them on numerous occasions, trying to guide them as they sought a brighter future for the farm. It was difficult to keep them focused as the discussions and arguments fluctuated between financial and relationship issues and often devolved into anything but resolving issues.

And then one morning at 8:00 a.m. my phone rang. I saw it was Jim calling, which I found rather strange. I normally did not get phone calls from him that early. I was going to make a smart comment when I answered, but for some reason I didn't. When I said hello, all he said is, "he's dead." I was somewhat confused and asked him what he meant.

Jim had gone to his dad's place to pick him up for a long-awaited meeting with their lawyer. I suppose all the stress of the farm situation had caught up to Jack and he had died in his sleep.

I had chatted with Jack twice the day before. He called me out of sheer frustration over how long the process was taking, how others just did not see the urgency of getting their plan formalized. He wanted to move beyond the struggles of the past and craved a brighter future.

Although it's safe to say that the death of a loved one is never timely, Jack's came at a time when the farm was going through a major restructure. Suddenly the months of planning were for naught. The plan had to change.

Because of the financial situation, the current creditors and lenders wanted out. So Jim had to start planning a new strategy. Jack's estate had significant equity, and as a beneficiary, Jim was going to inherit much of that. The unsecured debt, which was going to be dealt with by a trustee in bankruptcy, now had to be addressed in a different way. There would have to be a restructure of debt.

It seemed that any and all attempts to get some sort of financing package together just were not working out. But Jim was persistent. I had numerous conversations with him during that time. I found it particularly difficult to balance my advice between optimism and realism. Based on my experience, I knew lenders

Chapter 9   Can We All Just Get Along? Turning Judgement to Curiosity

would be hesitant to provide the necessary financing. At the same time, I wanted to be encouraging.

After six lenders had turned him down, I simply thought he would have to restructure the farm by selling assets to improve his balance sheet. But Jim did not give up and went to see a seventh lender.

Jim let me know that the banker was coming for a tour of his farm. He called me that day and said he felt optimistic. Two days later when my phone rang, and I recognized his number, I wanted to let it go to voicemail. I just could not bear to simply hear him say he had been turned down again.

However, I did answer the call and was more than surprised to hear him tell me that he had been approved. That was a significant turning point for Jim. He could now start concentrating on running his business.

Jim has always been an entrepreneur. Not willing to just sit back and farm his land, he is always looking for other opportunities. He had dabbled with different ideas, and at the time of his dad's passing they had their grain farm but were also growing alfalfa to sell feed into the United States. Over time, Jim adapted to changing markets and today he operates a few different enterprises.

Jim has never been averse to seeking professional help. Starting with a mediator, he has also sought business advice from others. That included business advisers, lawyers, accountants, change managers, and strategic planners, among others. In 2013 he asked some of his closer advisers to sit on an advisory board. That gave him the opportunity to seek input on his business and assist in developing new plans and strategies.

But Jim was always more than a businessperson. He had incredible insights into what other people were experiencing. As much as I have often said that he was a client of mine, and I have sometimes suggested he is my surrogate son, Jim has also been a good friend.

One day, as I showed up for an advisory board meeting, I was not in a good place. I had had an exceptionally difficult morning in a mediation. I managed to chair the meeting that afternoon, but after the meeting I quickly left to go home. By the time I got home I had received a text and a voicemail from Jim. He had recognized that I was not my normal self and was reaching out, checking in, and suggesting I give him a call if I needed to talk about it.

Over the course of the last number of years I have had various challenges and opportunities come my way. Jim and I would have coffee and a chat on a regular basis. During those chats we would exchange war stories, our ups and downs since the last time we had met. He was always curious about my life and over time has provided significant input and advice for me. It is always appreciated. I look forward to many more of those chats as we both navigate the challenges and opportunities that come our way.

Takeaway

Conflict is a normal part of life. Whether with our partners, kids, other family members, colleagues, neighbours, or others, we will experience times when there is disagreement. How we deal with that conflict is integral to how our relationships can not only be maintained but also grow.

People have a tendency to become entrenched in their ideas and opinions. And as such, they will stand on their point to their dying day. We see that all around us. All things Covid brought that out. We see it in theological debates. It's never more obvious than when we follow politics. We can expand that list to include numerous social issues that currently take centre stage. As that happens, what started as a minor disagreement can become full-blown conflict. We believe we have the ability and right to declare who is right and who is wrong. And, of course, we are always right

Chapter 9   Can We All Just Get Along? Turning Judgement to Curiosity

and the other is always wrong. Relationships are broken, families torn apart, and communities cast into turmoil.

Left unresolved, conflict has the potential to become a bigger problem. It festers and creates uncomfortable feelings. We construct narratives to try to make sense of it. Often those narratives become stories that define us. And as someone once suggested to me, up to 50 percent of what we remember didn't happen the way we think it did, so people end up being angry and bitter about things that are but figments of their imagination.

Reality is often so intricate that it can give rise to equally valid yet seemingly contradictory viewpoints. In such situations, we often find ourselves becoming defensive, especially when confronted with ideas that challenge our preconceived notions. Defensiveness is a natural behavioural response triggered by a perceived threat or an attack on our self-esteem or identity. It's our way of preserving our self-image, and to do so, we instinctively push back.

One of my favorite conflict resolution tips is that we must learn to turn judgement to curiosity. Nothing comes easier, and is often somewhat enjoyable, than being judgemental. When we look at world events, when we hear political discourse, when we scroll through social media, and even in conversations with colleagues or those we love, we tend to be judgemental when we see or hear something we do not agree with.

Turning that judgement to curiosity will help avoid destructive conflict. Curiosity will lead to understanding. I often tell my clients at the outset of mediation that the first step needs to be understanding. It's not about establishing blame or figuring out who is right and who is wrong. It's interesting how often parties, through building understanding, change their perspective on the conflict they are dealing with and are able to begin the process of proactively seeking resolution.

It is also important to understand that there is no shame in reaching out for help when we experience unresolved conflict. I often get calls from folks who are looking for help. As we discuss the issues they are dealing with, it comes to light that the conflict has been ongoing for years. Those situations can be difficult because the longer the conflict remains unresolved, the more tension there is. Emotions tend to overshadow objectivity. They have constructed narratives, becoming more entrenched in their positions. Being proactive will lead to better relationships. And there are those that can help you, you don't have to go it alone.

Chapter 10
Talking About it Helps: A Passion for Mental Wellness in Agriculture

I am being led into a dark studio knowing I am about to go on a live, call-in radio show. We've been invited to discuss the upcoming workshops I'll be facilitating, aimed at addressing the often-hidden topic of men and depression. The show begins, the host introduces us, and then looks at me and says, "I understand you have a story to tell." A moment of panic sets in. I have an adrenaline rush, never has time moved so slowly. I have a choice. I can shut up and look idiotic. Or I can start talking.

In 2007, as our farm was winding down, I came across an ad in the *Manitoba Cooperator* calling for volunteers for the Manitoba Farm and Rural Stress Line (MFRSL) as it was called at the time. That caught my attention. I thought that as an extension to my mediation work, getting the training for intensive counselling could be a good thing. Furthermore, I felt, based on my own experiences, I had something to offer.

My wife and I talked about it and decided we would both apply. The folks at the MFRSL were somewhat concerned about a husband and wife being in training at the same time. However, they accepted both of us, and that marked the beginning of my journey of discovery.

The person who did the intake interview at the MFRSL and the subsequent training became a close friend in later years. For a period, I had an office across the hall from the farm line, and we would spend time talking about our individual life experiences. We would chat about the need for more mental wellness resources for our agricultural community. I know she has certainly helped me in my journey, and I hope in some small way I have helped her as well.

I chuckle at times when I think back to the first training session. One of the exercises we did was meant to teach us how to have awkward conversations. We had to stand face to face with another participant and as we stood there, the trainer gave us topics that each of us had to talk about for one minute. I ended up being partnered with a woman somewhat older than me. The first topic that was given to us was masturbation. Needless to say, things became awkward in a real hurry. To this day I have no clue what I said, which is probably best, and I do not remember what this woman, rather uncomfortably, said to me. What I do know is that she dropped out of the training after that evening. I hope it wasn't something I said.

Together with the training I received for the MFRSL and further training for trauma and crisis response, I came to a better understanding of mental health. As with my conflict resolution training, I was able to apply the training to life experiences from the past. That helped me in better understanding, but also became an important component for the discovery piece of my journey.

In early 2008 I began my volunteering, answering calls on the farm line, the Manitoba crisis line, and the suicide line. The instructions were clear. For the first number of shifts we would be supervised by another counsellor. Shortly after my first shift began the phone rang on the crisis line and my supervising counsellor answered it. As she talked to the caller, the farm line rang. I knew I should not answer it

Chapter 10 Talking About it Helps

till the other counselor could listen in. She was quite engrossed in her call, so I took it upon myself to answer the farm line without supervision. After all, what could possibly go wrong?

Within seconds, I recognized the voice of the caller. This caller had called me previously enquiring about the mediation work I do and whether I might be able to help her with some farm relational issues. This created a dilemma for me. Do I let on who I am, or do I carry on the conversation anonymously?

Finally I admitted to the caller who I was. Turned out she didn't mind, and we ended up with a good conversation. We discussed the stress of familial conflict, the generational differences and how those impacted working together and making business decisions. We talked about how financial struggles added to the tensions. And then we were able to chat about the options available to the family to overcome some of the challenges.

In 2010 the manager at the MFRSL informed us that the United Way would be sponsoring a series of workshops on men and depression and that they were looking for someone to facilitate these workshops. I was asked whether I would be interested. I suggested that I would need to think about it. After some thought, I decided that I could not see myself doing that, so I called the farm line to let the manager know. She was not available, so I told the person who answered the call, the same one that had trained me for the work on the crisis lines, that she could pass on a message to the manager that I would be declining the offer. In her wisdom, she did not pass on that message but rather told the manager that I would do it. I think I still owe her for that.

After I reluctantly consented to doing the facilitation, the manager said that she really wanted a farmer to share his story of farming and mental health challenges, and wondered if I knew someone that would do that. Nobody came to mind. After a day or two she, being familiar with my journey, asked me whether I would tell my story. Without second thought I said yes. I seem to have a couple of issues in my life. First, I will often say yes without giving thought to the implications of my answer. And when I do say no, as I tried to do with the workshop facilitation, I am still easily manipulated.

As it turned out, I co-facilitated along with a psychologist. My job was to talk about recognizing the various stressors in farming, offer some thoughts on how to deal with that stress, and then share my own story. I gave considerable thought to how I could link those. Interestingly enough, I still wasn't considering the implications of sharing my story.

The kickoff to the workshops was a call-in radio show. Just that morning, I had participated in my first interview where I was asked very specific questions about my mental illness. I still felt a little raw about that. That interview was for a newspaper, so I didn't feel quite as vulnerable as when the host of the radio show asked me to start telling my story to a live audience.

The moment of truth hit. You know that feeling when your life flashes before your eyes? At the time that was an "oh crap" moment, today I would probably suggest it was a "wtf" moment. Whatever the case, I knew I could either shut up and look totally idiotic or begin talking. I began talking. I cannot emphasize enough how much talking about my journey has helped me, whether with my family, friends, neighbours, colleagues or others.

I was rather surprised at how many people approached me and shared about their own journeys. I came to a quick understanding that we all are on a journey and that many of us encounter challenges. I also learned quickly that when we talk to each other, we learn from each other. And it is with conversations like that, we find the encouragement to move forward. That also encouraged me to continue telling my story. That solidified my passion.

Recently I was involved in an interview where I was asked what my lived experiences taught me about the power of humour when it comes to talking about mental wellness. After all, the interviewer

Chapter 10   Talking About it Helps

said, your website describes you as a humourist. There you go. The good news was it was not a live interview, so I had some time to reflect on that.

By definition, a humourist is a writer or speaker who shares amusing stories about funny situations or experiences. It's easy to understand this concept. Moreover, in discussions about mental health, even a serious speaker or writer might incorporate humour to alleviate the tension that often arises as people grapple with their place in these conversations.

Humour, while often a source of lightheartedness and connection, can sometimes be used in unhealthy ways. I've been reminded on occasion that my attempts at humour are not always suitable in specific situations. At times, I've employed humour as a coping mechanism to shield myself from painful emotions. In my past, laughter has served as a camouflage for feelings of hurt, fear, anger, or disappointment. I've even resorted to self-deprecating humour, using it as a defense mechanism to conceal moments of low self-esteem. And yes, I've been guilty of using humour to mislead people, offering them a humorous façade to divert their attention from what was truly happening within me, a way of saying, "laugh at this, so you won't see the deeper struggles I'm facing."

However, laughter can be a powerful antidote for stress, pain, and conflict. Based on research, nothing works faster to bring your emotions back into balance than a good laugh. It lightens our burdens; it inspires us and builds connections with others. Research has shown that kids laugh up to four hundred times a day. As adults, that can drop to as low as ten. That means we must learn to laugh more.

Early in my journey of recovery, I was sitting alone and watching a sitcom. I laughed aloud at something that was said. My daughter stuck her head in the room and asked whether I was okay. I gave her a puzzled look and wondered about her question. She told me she had never heard me laugh out loud before. That saddened me.

As much as I thought I had always had a sense of humour, I clearly had lost something in my mental health deterioration.

When I first started talking publicly about my journey, there was limited interest. I did a few interviews, talked to a few groups, but the topic quickly died. Clearly there was still a significant stigma involved, and so the interest waned. In later years, that interest resurfaced and interest in mental health, particularly as it concerns our agricultural community, has grown. The invitations to present have increased, and it has become easier to get folks engaged in the conversation.

I have always approached my presentations with a certain trepidation. I have found it is important to be able to share openly but also make sure the language I use is one that others can relate to.

In a presentation I did to the organization that I once was president of, I spoke freely about a couple of issues that were and continue to be a component of stress management. One of the areas I frequently cover is what stress can do to our physical beings. Of note, that evening I mentioned that men, dealing with mental health issues, often experience erectile dysfunction. Because that can be a touchy subject, I try and use some levity. I referred to an episode of a comedy show I used to enjoy. In the scene I referenced, a gentleman is sharing with a friend about some issues he is experiencing in his love life. The advice she gives him provides a chuckle but also makes the point. She in essence tells him that; "if your mind is iffy, you can't get a stiffy."

The following day a participant got up during the meeting and voiced his outrage about what I had spoken about. As I knew this gentleman quite well, I phoned him to talk about this. I approached that with defensiveness rather than curiosity, so the conversation did not go well. He was quite adamant that bedroom issues needed to stay in the bedroom. I suspect that a contributing factor to our mental health is the fact that, too often, we feel that our issues should stay in the bedroom or the closet. But I digress.

Chapter 10   Talking About it Helps

The irony is that I had used the above analogy in another setting and the day following someone had phoned a crisis line, said he had heard me say this, and wondered whether that was true as that was something he was experiencing.

In my presentation, I had also shared the story about my wife suggesting she had been married to four different men and how two of them she would have preferred not to experience. The same gentleman was rather chagrined and suggested that was not something to make light of. Excuse me? He went on to say that Tiger Woods—this was during the time it came to light that he had been involved with numerous women—had shown us how that subject was not one that should be talked about. I don't think he was listening to what, at the time, was a rather sensitive part of my journey.

Being an overly sensitive type and wanting to make sure that I spoke correctly and appropriately in future presentations, I sought counsel from others, including a counsellor, a colleague, and the manager of a crisis line, wondering whether I had been out of line. Each one of them assured me that it was important to talk about those things, and I need not feel bad.

As opportunities to present increased, I found it necessary to refine my approach to communication. I discovered that each generation has its unique methods for handling conflict and stress, prompting me to recognize and respect these differences to effectively convey my message. There were instances where my humor missed the mark, or my language proved inappropriate for certain audiences. Additionally, I realized that I occasionally resorted to sweeping generalizations. Through personal growth in my presentation style, I've developed a deeper comprehension of why certain remarks may have caused offense to others.

In a presentation to a group of young entrepreneurs, I talked about conflict and stress particularly as it concerns those that work closely with their partners/spouses. I approached the subject from my own perspective, perhaps somewhat influenced by having grown up in a different time when gender roles were more clearly defined. But I also based it on what I had observed with many couples I have dealt with in my conflict management work.

After that presentation I received some emails suggesting there is not a dichotomy between men and women and that I was sexist and didn't understand relationships. That was greatly concerning for me. Although I don't believe that I am sexist, and I think I have some experience with relationships, I needed to better understand that the younger generations approach relationships differently than I do and my approach, real or perceived, was undermining their own identities, roles and cultural norms.

A typical part of my presentations often involves weaving in personal anecdotes from my own journey. I find it highly effective to illustrate the different concepts and theories related to stress and conflict management using my own experiences as examples. While I'm generally open about sharing my journey, there are moments when my emotions become quite evident. To navigate through such instances, I rely on humor—it not only helps me keep my emotions in check but also aids the audience as they grapple with how their journeys fit into the narrative.

Some years ago, I was asked to be part of a panel to discuss farm stress. My role was to be somewhat different than normal, as I was asked to just focus on my own story. In typical fashion, when I agreed to that, I gave little to no thought of what I was committing to. As the time came closer, I had an inkling that I might be in for a challenge. So instead of freewheeling it, like I normally would, I decided to write out the entire presentation and just read it.

As I wrote out my story, I became keenly aware that I was drilling deeper into my past than I had before. There were pieces that brought out emotions that I had not expected. So I had a feeling that presenting this in front of two hundred people could well overwhelm me. I was not wrong. It turned out to be the most difficult presentation I have ever made. I found myself significantly outside my comfort zone.

Chapter 10   Talking About it Helps

When I reflected on that experience, I felt various emotions. I felt vulnerable but that's okay. I was quite emotional before, during and after. That's okay too. The response from people was incredible, which was awesome. And, as per usual, the part I liked best was others coming to validate what I had said, share their own experiences, or ask for help for others that were traveling a similar journey as my own. It reiterated what I keep saying. We need to *talk about it!*

In large part, because of responses like that, my passion for mental wellness in agriculture has grown over the years. With my own experiences, and the response when I talk about them, I see that there is so much more that needs to be done to spread the word and build on mental wellbeing resources for the agricultural community.

I suppose that is why I jumped at the opportunity when I received a phone call in early 2021 to be involved in establishing a farmer mental wellness program in Manitoba. Some background work had already been done. Similar programs were being run on Prince Edward Island and in a few counties in Ontario with good uptake.

In my mind this should be relatively simple. It should be easy enough to find some funding. After all, the topic of mental health in agriculture was gaining traction, so that meant there would be groups and organizations ready to write a cheque. In addition, I knew one or two counsellors that would probably be interested in providing services.

As it turns out, it was somewhat more complicated than that. But if you have the right people involved, it can make a complicated situation easier. In October of 2021 we formed a not-for-profit called the Manitoba Farmer Wellness Program. Based on anecdotal evidence, the program needed to be flexible, fully confidential, free to farm families, and have farm-focused professionals delivering the services. And we were able to deliver on that.

I have been asked on numerous occasions whether I would have utilized the services of a program such as this when I was experiencing my mental health crisis when I was farming. The answer is an unequivocal yes. When you read about my experiences in seeking professional help and some of the frustrations I had, it will make sense that I would have welcomed this type of service. For me this program is a dream come true.

Takeaway

Farming has changed dramatically over the years. When I think back to when my father farmed and compare that to farming today, the differences are astronomical. Farmers have more and more options available to them, requiring more and more decisions. Many other issues, such as mother nature, government policies, commodity pricing and others, are out of their control.

A 2016 survey done out of the University of Guelph showed some alarming results. Of the 1100 farmers surveyed, 45% reported high levels of stress, compared with 27% in the general population. The number that really hit home with me was that 58% of respondents met the criteria for an anxiety classification. That simply means if they were to seek help from a professional, they would be diagnosed with an anxiety disorder.[1]

In a 2021 follow-up survey, 76% of farmers said they were currently experiencing moderate or high perceived stress. The survey revealed that suicide ideation was two times higher in farmers than in the general population. One in four Canadian farmers felt their life was not worth living, wished they were dead or had thought of taking their own life in the previous 12 months. In addition, there was an increase in alcohol use as a coping mechanism.[2]

---

1 *Farmers Need, Want Mental Health Help: Survey*, https\\:news.uoguelph.ca/2016/06/farmers-need-want-mental-health-help-survey/
2 *Farmers' Mental Health Worsened during Pandemic, OVC Study Finds*, https\\:ovc.uoguelph.ca/news/node/897.

Chapter 10 Talking About it Helps

To a degree, these results normalize my own experiences. And perhaps, normalize is not the right term to use. However, it provides me with a better understanding of why I experienced what I did. But it also paints a picture of the ongoing challenges in agriculture. A combination of that and my own journey have driven my passion for mental wellness in agriculture. In my way of thinking, mental health is every bit as important as physical health. But due to stigma and a lack of understanding of the intricacies of mental health, we tend to ignore the signs and symptoms of deteriorating mental wellness.

Over the years I have witnessed an increased momentum in addressing the stress, and by extension the mental health, that farm families face. That has provided the impetus to continue to work in this field. Having the ability to connect with like minded folks across the country has been encouraging and exciting. Just recently I was involved in a national symposium to chat about various programs that are available. There was discussion on what steps could be taken to further reduce stigma, to ensure farmers and their families would avail themselves of the resources that are available, and to talk about research in mental health and agriculture. Events like these inspire me and further fuel my passion for mental wellness in agriculture.

As a result of ongoing and increasing stress in agriculture, we now have organizations such as the Canadian Centre for Agricultural Wellbeing and the Do More Agriculture Foundation which provide resources for mental health in agriculture on a national level. There are provincial initiatives, such as the Manitoba Farmer Wellness Program, that provide counselling for our agricultural producers, their families and employees. This work needs to continue and grow. Because without the farmer there is no farm.

Chapter 11
Who Am I?
A Piece of the Puzzle, But Where Does It Fit?

The meeting was to start at noon and consisted of myself and ten other professional mediators along with the organization we were contracted with. I was nervous as I sat down and looked around the room. Any confidence I had prior to walking in dissipated. Who was I, I questioned, to be part of this group of professional, self-assured individuals? In the midst of discussions, I often restrained myself, hesitating to contribute. Regret weighed heavily each time an idea I had thought of went unspoken, only to be suggested by someone else. When I did muster the courage to speak, nervousness caused me to stumble over words. In those moments I felt like an outsider, convinced that I simply did not belong.

In certain life situations I am told that admitting it, when you struggle with something, is the first step in a process, a process of healing, or a process for change. As you have read about in previous chapters, I was often filled with doubts as I got involved in various opportunities. So I will admit it. I live with imposter

Chapter 11 Who Am I? A Piece of the Puzzle, But Where Does It Fit?

syndrome. Knowing what I know now, I have been living with this for most of my life, perhaps even *all* my life.

I only became familiar with imposter syndrome later in life. Some years ago, I was visiting a friend at his cottage. As we sat and shared war stories about life and work, I confided in him that I felt completely out of sorts with my life and my career. I didn't feel like I fit in. I felt like I didn't belong. I questioned my abilities as a husband, a father, a friend, a professional. I questioned whether I had the ability to perform my work.

Yes, my work was going okay. I was relatively busy mediating. I had just started working for another organization which included other mediators. I shared with him the story at the beginning of this chapter. When that group would meet, I would find myself shrinking away from being involved in the discussions because I was convinced that I did not belong, I did not have the knowledge, education, and experience of these other professionals. Although, in retrospect, I suspect I had the knowledge and experience, just not the confidence to show it.

When I confided in my friend about my thoughts, I explained it by suggesting that I was hoping to succeed before anyone found out about my self-perceived inabilities. He had a smile on his face when he told me two things. First, he assured me he knew all too well how I felt because he experienced the same self-doubts as I did. It was oddly reassuring to hear he lived with the same condition, after all he is well educated with a good career. Secondly, he claimed to have a name for it: imposter syndrome. At the time I was convinced that he was making this up but when I did research on it, I found out he was right.

In simple terms, imposter syndrome occurs when, even if you've achieved success, you still feel like you're not up to the task. Any accomplishments you have are clouded by self-doubt, making you feel like you're pretending to be something you're not. This inner struggle involves being quite hard on yourself. It usually happens when your self-esteem is low, constantly measuring yourself against others, being overly sensitive, and avoiding social situations. Interestingly it's often linked to a more widespread anxiety disorder.

I think that describes me quite well, both professionally and personally. And that got me thinking about other areas of my life. Think about it. A salesman suggests that I had never been a farmer. When I became chairman of Manitoba Pork, I felt that others' trust in me was misplaced. When I thought about parenthood, I felt like I had come up way short. When I began sharing the story of my journey with mental illness, I wondered why anyone would care. When I became a mediator, I felt out of my realm.

Just recently I attended my doctor's office as I needed to complete my annual physical. I use the term "annual" loosely as I have yet to actually have an annual physical completed. For quite some time, it was every five years and now it is every three years. Why you may ask? That is what is required to maintain my Class 1 drivers' licence, a requirement for driving semis.

I have always been somewhat afraid of what a doctor might discover, should they actually run some tests. So I avoid the doctor's office as much as possible. This last go-around was not much different than others. The usual prodding, poking, blood tests, the dreaded poop test to be done at home and of course the prostate exam. I always feel bad for the doctor when the rubber glove comes on and they do what they have to do. However, when he told me that things "felt okay" up there I certainly did not ask for a second opinion.

I apologized to the doctor for making him do this, but he laughed it off, said it was no different than getting an oil change done on my car. That made me laugh because I avoid doing that as well. Perhaps for the same reasons I don't like going to the doctor. It seems that every time I take my car for something as simple as

Chapter 11 Who Am I? A Piece of the Puzzle, But Where Does It Fit?

an oil change, I leave having spent a small fortune on all the things they seem to find wrong with my car.

In the past, when I left the doctor's office after a complete physical, I had been told that if they found anything nefarious, they would be in contact. This time the doctor told me right off the bat that I should make a follow-up appointment. That immediately made me think something might be seriously wrong. So for the next three weeks I worried about what my diagnosis could potentially be.

The night before the follow-up appointment, my wife asked about my schedule for the following day. I informed her that I was going to the doctor to find out how long I had left to live. When I told my doctor about that conversation, he laughed and said I was good for another 100,000 miles but that I should avoid speeding. That worked for me till I left and began to wonder what that really meant. That made me curious about how many miles this body of mine had already put on. I needed to know that to get any assurance from the doctor's comments. I suppose it's all relative.

Shortly after that appointment we got together with some family. I told them about my appointment and what the doctor had said. One of them, in a cynical tone, asked how the doctor would know that I had 100,000 miles left. Without hesitation I said that the doctor had stuck his finger up my butt, literally been in touch with my inner self, so knew more about me than I knew about myself. Quite simple actually, at least in my way of thinking.

However, I digress. For a number of years, I had wondered why I kept my Class 1 drivers licence. Quite frankly, I have not driven a semi since 1983. For years I kept the license because it forced me to go for a physical. But then, through time, I began to question why. Prior to my last notification that it was time for a physical, I had lunch with a friend. When I told him about my thoughts, he told me his dad had always said that as long as you have a Class 1 drivers licence you will never be out of a job. So I hustled back to the doctor.

And that's when I had an epiphany. The reason I was keeping my Class 1 licence was because it gave me a fallback, just in case I would ever find myself unemployed. I was a professional mediator and stress management specialist. I had been involved in various training to become better at what I did. I had found significant success over the years but kept being full of doubt. I often felt like a fraud. And so, I needed a fallback. That was my imposter syndrome kicking in.

That got me going down that rabbit hole even further. One day as I was chatting with my kids, I made the comment that if I were to die, they wouldn't miss a beat. I know, that sounds like I am on a "poor, pitiful me" trip. But really, it wasn't. It was my imposter syndrome rearing its ugly head. I did not feel I had been an accomplished father so what would it matter if I was gone? To me it seemed that their lives were in order. They were healthy, they had good jobs, and they had a good mother who had done most of the parenting as I was gone so much.

Their reaction left me surprised. Contrary to my assumptions, they firmly asserted that I held significant importance in their lives. They reminisced about cherished moments and recounted the positive impact I'd made on their lives. They expressed the desire to have me watch their children grow, for all of us to spend time together.

In spite of being told that I am a good parent, being told that I am a good mediator, being told that my story has had an impact, the feeling lingers. That means I have to change the narrative happening in my brain on a constant basis. Perhaps I am not an imposter. Perhaps I can let go of my Class 1 licence. Then again, I might never go for another physical if I did that.

And then I took a minute to reflect on the meeting I mentioned at the outset. I thought about what had been said. I realized that

Chapter 11 Who Am I? A Piece of the Puzzle, But Where Does It Fit?

many of the "novel" ideas that were shared, I was already practicing. I came to understand that I was good at my job. I softened my view of myself. I opened my heart and my mind. And in the same way I would have responded if someone else had told me that, I started feeling better about myself. I felt validated. I felt worthy. Worthy of the kindness and respect I was showing myself. The kindness and respect I deserve.

Takeaway

It has sometimes been suggested that life is like a puzzle. Each piece therein represents the various experiences we have. And all put together, the pieces form a picture of our life.

As such, as individuals, we have a tendency to form that picture in our mind and work on putting the pieces together. That creates challenges as the picture we have in our minds isn't reality, it's fiction. We may want that picture to be our life but our experiences through life may well change that.

In essence, we are putting together a puzzle without knowing what the final image will be. It's difficult to know where the pieces go. It's difficult to know what some pieces represent. And when you lack clarity on who you are meant to be or what your life was meant to be, it's difficult to put pieces together. We begin to question ourselves. But if you take a minute and honestly ask yourself, would you like you if you met you, I suspect the answer would be yes.

Imposter syndrome adds to the challenge of piecing it all together. You have the pieces, but they don't seem to fit. You look at other folks around you and want similar pieces as they have. You force pieces together because you don't feel comfortable with yourself. And, certainly in my case, we need constant validation to gain a sense of comfort with the pieces we have and where they go. I find that having just one person tell me "You've got this," provides the energy and courage to carry on.

At times we also become frustrated with the puzzle. It seems to be taking far too long to complete. We don't like the picture that is taking shape. We fall into this false hope that we can only find happiness when the puzzle is complete, and all the pieces fit. We forget about those around us who help and support.

We must always keep in mind that the puzzle we are working on is a process. The final picture may be the destination, but to get there remains a journey. The goal is to be the best version of yourself. And when you are the best version of yourself it will become easier to identify puzzle pieces and know where they belong.

As humans, we possess an innate desire to be understood by others, particularly during periods of distress. We never outgrow that. Our pain and anxiety are reduced the more others understand and care. Our physical and mental health improve when others show they care, when they show they understand, when they reach out to help. Using that same principle on ourselves is just as important. This is where self-compassion is so important. We need to better understand ourselves. We need to be kinder to ourselves. We need to be able to reach out and help ourselves. And as we do that, it will be easier to feel confident with who you are and where the puzzle pieces go.

Chapter 12
The Journey: Weathering the Storm

It's Christmas, and we have taken our kids skiing in the Rockies. What a feeling of security. Surrounded by mountains, it's easy to forget about the relentless demands of life. Nobody can get me here. I have fun, and I feel relaxed. But then it's time to go home. And as we leave the mountains and hit the flat prairie, reality hits. There are only a few days left in the year to complete our year-end and to figure out how to operate for the next year. There is a pending lawsuit from a feed company. I know there is significant work to be done on the farm. My anxiety spikes and a feeling of dread hits me as I think about the challenges awaiting me on the farm and in the year ahead.

In my introduction I refer to my mental health as a journey. Simply put, a journey involves traveling from point A to point B, encompassing a series of events—some positive, some challenging. It carries with it memories that shape our experiences. As you know by now, I like using the word labyrinth to describe my journey. It's a path with twists and turns where moving forward should be relatively easy but, at times, becomes more difficult as we reflect and get caught up in our life experiences.

If I use the journey definition above, that means I need to have a starting point. This becomes rather difficult, as it is not that simple. As I alluded to earlier, after my diagnosis, I spent considerable time analyzing the starting point of my journey with mental illness. As much as I was diagnosed in 2004, much of what I will share happened prior to that.

I now also suspect that my anxiety started at a young age. I could recall having deep anxiety as a teenager. At the time, largely due to my upbringing, I was convinced I was dealing with guilt. But no matter how much I would confess, and try and do the right thing, that internal churning continued. As I progressed with age, that anxiety would often rear its head. In certain situations, at work or at home, the anxiety could be debilitating.

When I first began speaking publicly about my mental health, or lack thereof, there was some interest from media. The first interview I did was with a reporter I knew well. She had interviewed me numerous times in the previous twenty years, but never about something as personal as my mental illness. I was somewhat apprehensive, but also curious, as I waited for the article to be published.

Her words, in describing me, are indelibly etched in my mind. "On the outside, he was a successful Wawanesa-area farmer and well-known pork industry leader. On the inside, he was drowning in a black hole." In my mind that was a good description of who I was. Although the part of being "a successful . . . farmer" is a little suspect, I had been drowning in a black hole.

Sometimes I find it difficult to describe my experience. I have heard at least four speakers describe anxiety and depression as being scared and tired at the same time. It's the fear of failure, but no urge to be productive. It's wanting friends but hating socializing. It's wanting to be alone but not wanting to be lonely. It's caring about everything, then caring about nothing. It's feeling everything at once, then feeling paralyzingly numb. Perhaps with that description it will be easier to understand as I talk about my journey.

Chapter 12   The Journey: Weathering the Storm

Just over a year after my initial diagnosis and going on medication, I made the decision to go off the meds. I cannot recall why I made that decision, but it is something we often hear about. People go on meds, think they are doing fine, and then go off them, only to find out it was, in fact, the meds that were making them feel fine. I suppose I fell into that same line of thinking.

Combined with my mental health issues and ongoing and increasing stress, my behaviours started changing. Of particular note was an increase in expectations for myself and for others. I could do nothing right, and neither could anyone else in my life. Building meaningful relationships became difficult due to those increased expectations, because those increased expectations would get in the way. And that led to tension and conflict.

For as long as I can remember I have been an overthinker. My imposter syndrome, my low self-esteem, and my mental illness just added to it. So any type of disagreement or comments made by others would send my thoughts into overdrive. As a result, I would shrink back into my shell. That left me with a choice. Either talk about it and mess things up further, or not say anything and let it eat away at me on the inside.

I began to notice a pattern of dissociation within myself, feeling increasingly disconnected not only from my own sense of identity but also from those around me. This disconnection manifested as a struggle with indecisiveness and a tendency to procrastinate, making even simple decisions feel overwhelming. Processing information became difficult, increasing the sense of helplessness and hopelessness that filled my thoughts and emotions.

Internally my self-esteem reached new lows. I felt that I could do nothing right. I spent an inordinate amount of time trying to find someone to blame for everything that was going wrong. And my mind was constantly in rumination phase. I often compare my anxiety to a squirrel. Imagine a squirrel. Very active. Quite noisy. Flits from place to place. Never runs in a straight line. Hops from tree to tree. Quite agile. Can be intrusive. Always on the lookout. Never a dull moment.

And just like that squirrel, anxiety created a myriad of thoughts running through my mind. As I dealt with one thought, another one came rushing in, scurrying about in my grey matter, jumping from one thought to another. It put me on edge. I became spooked, never knowing what waited around the next corner.

My coping mechanisms were not particularly helpful. For some time I had found that alcohol does an amazing job in easing anxiety. Unfortunately as alcohol leaves the body it increases anxiety, so when I came off the buzz, my anxiety increased exponentially. The only way to combat that was to drink more, which I did. And if it wasn't a self-medicated fog, it was finding other means of escaping.

I found the hog barn to be a sanctuary. Away from people, away from my phone, away from my family, and, perhaps, even an attempt to escape from myself. There were moments when the most challenging aspect of my anxiety and depression was my constant yearning to be anywhere but where I currently found myself. Yet when I finally reached another place, the urge to relocate once more would resurface. It left me pondering whether I was in pursuit of something or if, in fact, something was relentlessly pursuing me.

I found myself being easily irritated. I was quick to anger. That led to increased tension with my brother, my wife, and my kids. As that tension increased, there was more conflict. With the increase in conflict, my anxiety skyrocketed, and the depression deepened. That led to detachment, I didn't want to be around people.

I now understand the challenges my wife, kids, and brother faced. It is difficult living and working with someone who is experiencing anxiety and depression. Because of a distorted way of thinking, the depressed person is constantly questioning relationships. They tend to blame everyone around them for the increased tension. As much as others would like to help, that can become an

Chapter 12 The Journey: Weathering the Storm

impossible task. To try to maintain relationships becomes a matter of supporting as best possible, hoping that something will change.

Research has shown that stress impacts business decisions. In retrospect I understand the impact my stress and mental illness had on making business decisions. When I was feeling overwhelming stress and anxiety, my decisions were not rational. Instead of being based on sound, current information, I tended to make decisions based on what had produced positive outcomes in the past. And far too often I rushed the decisions because I just didn't want to think about it anymore.

Financial pressures were continuous. The hog price crash of '98 left us reeling, always trying to catch up. That meant making changes. It involved discussions with our lenders. We needed to adapt our production to a new reality.

We tried risk management tools that had just become available for hog producers. The first year, we locked in favourable prices for finished hogs. But as we know, markets can change in short order. Due to drought conditions across the prairies, feed grain prices skyrocketed. Then suddenly we were on the losing side again. And losses continued.

You will often hear farmers say, "there is always next year." I was operating on the belief that there was always next week, or next month, and for sure, there would be next year. But due to various factors, most of them outside our control, next year seemed to be a long way away. That involved difficult decisions. Often these decisions were made based on desperation rather than current and accurate market information. And as our cash flow suffered, we would compound the problem by marketing hogs that were not ready for market, which only added to lost revenue.

A simple task, such as going through the mail, was arduous. And often the mail, unopened, would end up lying on my desk for days. Very simply, I was avoiding the inevitable. As I learned during that time, avoiding just adds to worrying. And we know that worrying is letting your mind create something you don't want to have happen.

That really hit home for me one day when I was dealing with a farmer in farm debt mediation. As we were compiling his financial statements, I asked him about some custom work he had had done. He told me he had received the invoice two weeks prior but had never opened the envelope because he was worried about how much it would be. I told him he should open it and check the amount because he would start feeling better about it. He gave me a strange look but then complied. After he checked the amount, and in spite of it being more than expected, he looked at me and asked me how I had known that he would feel better about it. I pointed out that when he saw the amount his brain switched from worrying about it to actively figuring out a way to deal with it.

Later that day I decided that I needed to practice what I was preaching. I grabbed a stack of unopened envelopes and began opening them. Quickly I came across a registered letter. It was a statement of claim, registered by a feed company, suing for unpaid feed bills. I wish I could tell you that my brain switched from worrying as well. It didn't. It opened a whole new issue that created increased anxiety. I now needed to get a lawyer involved, knowing full well what the consequences could be.

To this day, Christmas is a struggle for me. When I was still farming, Christmas was in the last week of our fiscal year. That often meant that between celebrations with family and friends, we were hunkered down trying to finalize our year end. It meant budgeting for the next year. It usually involved some tense discussions on how to make things work. On top of that, the days were at their shortest and weather was normally quite cold, not a pleasant time to be dealing with livestock.

Although we both had our off-farm work, mine was based in the province so as much as I might not have been at the farm, I was still at the farm. So when it was time to talk to bankers, suppliers,

Chapter 12   The Journey: Weathering the Storm

and lawyers, the task often fell on me. To this day, as I travel the highways and byways of Manitoba, I see reminders of places I was when I would receive phone calls telling me our account was overdrawn or a feed bill had to be paid, or hogs were too light to be marketed, or equipment had broken down.

Due to the many hours I spent on the road doing anything except taking care of the farm meant that when I was home, I had to put in long hours to catch up and get ready for the next trip away. That often meant late nights at the barn hauling manure, moving pigs, and planning. To ease the pressure, those long days would often include alcohol.

With my involvement in agricultural politics, I met and chatted with countless other farmers. I always found it strange that it seemed we were struggling, but by all appearances very few others were. And then when we were selling pigs at a significant loss and others had utilized risk management programs and their returns were much better, I questioned my management abilities and with that my self-esteem took another hit.

I can only imagine the consequences social media would have had on my mental health. As much as one may be aware of the fallacies and false façades of social media, it can still create anxiety. One of my clients related to me how he had seen someone post that they had just made a final loan payment on a tractor a year ahead of schedule. That made him feel like a failure because he had just had to make arrangements to extend the loan on his tractor.

During the last seven years of farming, I was also dealing with farmers in farm debt mediation. Often during those mediation meetings or conversations around their kitchen tables, my mind was wandering. I knew that the issues I was helping others with were not different than what waited for me when I got home. So when the conversation would ultimately turn to options for resolution, there would be talk about downsizing, selling out, or even declaring bankruptcy. And then I would reflect on that as I went back to my own challenges, knowing full well that those conversations needed to happen on my farm as well.

In the presentations I do these days, I often talk about how our brain reacts to stress, anxiety, and depression. Although I could describe in some detail various components of our brain, such as the thalamus and the amygdala and the work they do, I like to dummy it down. In my way of thinking, we have two parts to our brain. There is the part that reacts rationally and the part that reacts irrationally.

When the brain reacts rationally, it has the capacity to methodically evaluate and reason through various options with precision. It is conscientious and remains impartial in its judgments. Conversely, when the brain reacts irrationally, it represents our emotions and tends to reach hasty conclusions. It frequently exhibits impulsiveness, inaccuracy, and an unfortunate inclination to overreact. Notably, in the presence of stress or anxiety, the irrational part of our brain has a tendency to take the lead, often acting before the rational part of the brain can intervene.

Some time ago I needed to deal with a subscription that we no longer wanted. I knew the renewal date was fast approaching and so my wife had asked me to call the company and make sure it was cancelled before a new charge would show up on our credit card. The irrational part of my brain was already beginning to take over before I even made the call.

When I did call, I went through the rigmarole of pressing various buttons to get to actually talking to a human. By the time someone came on the line, I was ready to blow a gasket. When that person was less than cooperative, at least in my way of thinking, things deteriorated quickly, to the point where they simply hung up on me. When my wife came home and asked whether I had made the call, I was quite agitated as I described what had happened. She calmly picked up the phone, called the company and

Chapter 12 The Journey: Weathering the Storm

within a few short minutes had the problem solved. She tends to be much better at using the rational part of her brain.

I came to realize that my tendency to use the irrational part of my brain had wielded excessive control over many of the farm-related challenges I had to confront. I often yielded because I could no longer bear to dwell on certain issues. Consequently, I would sell our hogs at whatever price or weight, simply to escape the constant worry. This avoidance strategy led to a state of denial, as I desperately tried to evade the harsh reality of our circumstances. My obsession with the impending downfall of our farm further compounded the problem, rendering me paralyzed with fear. Each decision seemed fraught with danger, fueling a sense of desperation and panic that coerced me into making choices under the oppressive weight of fear.

From the day we decided we needed to sell the farm; it was over two years before that happened. And as much as I was on medication again, the difficulties kept me from really addressing my mental health. A year prior to the conclusion of the farm, I made the comment to my wife that I would be okay to grab a suitcase and walk off the farm never to speak of it again. Let the creditors take whatever morsels were left. I was giving up. I was angry, depressed, cynical, and completely done. Thankfully, with my wife's encouragement, that did not happen, and within a year we were able to sell the farm and wind down operations in a relatively coherent manner.

I have reoccurring dreams about my farm. I dream that the feed has run out and no one took note and did something about it. I dream that the bank is hounding me for money, and so I ship pigs that are not heavy enough to garner premiums. I dream that the feed company is delivering feed, and they need money from me before they can unload, so they have to call my mother. I dream that I come into the barn and pigs have escaped their pens and are running loose and wreaking havoc. I dream that the person emptying my manure storage has pumped it on neighbouring yards and has created floods in their homes.

And then there is the dream I had where we had to buy back the farm because the people that had bought it changed their mind and did not want it anymore. In the meantime, I needed to load pigs to market them as I was depopulating the barn, but my brother had taken the truck so I couldn't hook up the trailer. And I knew that the pigs were too light and would not garner the kind of money I needed. In the meantime, I was showing the farm to another interested party, but at the same time, I had to load turkeys that had been injured when they were chased over a barb wire fence, which was discovered when the people interested in buying the farm wanted to see the valley behind the barns. Are you surprised I woke up feeling anxious?

One night I dreamt that I was going to the barn early in the morning. I have this sinking feeling that something is not right. As I walk in, I see the feed mill has broken down and there is grain piled high where it should not be. The realization hits, I have not been there for a few days so the pigs must be hungry. But wait, I thought the barn was empty. As I venture further into the barn, I hear a loud commotion. I look through the window and see pigs running around in the alleyway. They have pulled down the wire for my manure scraper. Small pigs are mixed with heavier pigs. The feeders are empty. How can this be? The bank has been calling. Our account is overdrawn. Surely there must be pigs ready to go. And then I wake up. It was all a bad dream.

Over time I had become aware that there were certain things that would trigger these types of dreams. As I sat and enjoyed my morning coffee, I tried to think back to what could have triggered the latest one. And then I remembered. A day earlier, I had met the banker with whom we were dealing as the farm was sinking deeper into a financial black hole. I wondered whether I needed to seek therapy for these recurring dreams. And then I thought that

Chapter 12   The Journey: Weathering the Storm

the banker probably needed therapy as well for having dealt with me and our situation.

Sometimes I wish that I would quit dreaming about the past. Although, when I do wake up and realize it was just a dream, I am filled with a profound relief, knowing those experiences are in the past, things I no longer need to concern myself with. It helps me understand better how life has changed for the good.

Let the dreams continue. They do cause momentary anxiety. But when I awake, I am filled with gratitude for what I have. Yes, my journey continues. Like the weather, I know my mental health will sometimes come with clouds or storms. But I also know that the sun will shine again, and I will feel the warmth. If not today, then tomorrow. Having rid myself of the farm finally gave me the opportunity to begin the healing process. I am not sitting here today to tell you that I became sick and have been healed. Rather I am telling you that I still walk in the labyrinth. But I am also telling you that because of a deeper understanding and utilizing what I have learned, it is much easier to keep moving forward in that journey.

Takeaway

It is no secret, although not always recognized, that stress has an effect on our mind, body, and emotions. There are a variety of ways that we can talk about stress, how stress can bring on anxiety and depression and how to find the right coping methods. Many years ago, when I was involved with the Manitoba Farm and Rural Stress Line, we used the analogy of weathering a storm.

Stress can become a full-blown crisis when a situation becomes so stressful that it breaks down one's ability to cope. All the tried and true ways of coping are no longer working. The body feels under attack. It responds by attempting to correct the imbalance. As that happens, anxiety increases and can easily lead to depression. It feels as if we have been *hit by the storm*. Many have come face to face with the realization that life will never be the same. Gone are the hopes and dreams for tomorrow. In many cases, people have lost what has taken generations to achieve. The pressure is relentless. It never seems to end. There are feelings of helplessness, shock, and anger. And somewhere in that storm people can lose their resilience.

After being hit by the storm, people often find themselves in *the foggy middle*. They have come to the realization that their life has changed. They may be experiencing a sense of loss of purpose, lifestyle, and identity. Common feelings include shock, disbelief, rage, or panic. They find themselves in a fog, feeling emptiness, confusion, and chaos, unsure which way to go. Nothing is clear. They need to find direction. Find the target. Find new coping methods. Gain a new understanding of how life has changed.

As people work their way through that foggy middle, they enter a recovery phase. They start to adjust to changing surroundings. They find themselves *on firm ground*. There is a return to a pre-crisis level of functioning.

It's a place where self-esteem, self-worth, and optimism increase. People often come face to face with the realization that what at one time had been a dream was not going to happen. They are forced to make changes. It may turn into a different way of life. But after the debilitating thoughts of failure and feelings of shame and guilt, they sense themselves regaining personal power.

I have had to learn new coping skills. My level of functioning is not what it once was. I seem to have a lower tolerance to stress. I need to remind myself of this on a regular basis. Otherwise, I find myself slipping back into old habits, back into a zone where coping is difficult. I can tell you that I know more about myself. I know what I want and most of all I know how to adapt. The challenge is to know that I know and ensure I act upon that knowledge.

Chapter 12   The Journey: Weathering the Storm

It becomes important to recognize stress and be as proactive as possible. The Chinese symbol for crisis consists of two words: danger and opportunity. Although it is very difficult to comprehend any type of opportunity when you are hit by the storm, that opportunity may well come. Through a process of "finding" yourself, through gaining new perspectives, focusing on solutions, adjustments can be made. And when that happens, it is possible to see new opportunities in the future. It is possible to weather the storm.

Chapter 13
My Addiction: Coming Out of the Closet

Awakening in the stillness of the early morning, the darkness outside feels as oppressive as the relentless anxiety that eats at my insides. I know there are a few hours left before I can find relief for the mind-numbing anxiety I am feeling. One minute I am cold, the next I am sweating. The shakes are uncontrollable. Never has time moved so slowly. I count the minutes, desperately hoping for morning to come. I need a drink. I need to soothe the anguish of my soul. The AC/DC song "Highway to Hell" is stuck in my head: a somewhat fitting theme song for my life at the time.

Although I may talk about it, writing about my addiction remains difficult. I hope that as my thoughts fall into place, they may create a deeper understanding of who I was and how I really longed for a peace of mind and spirit that just always seemed so elusive. And, in some small way, I hope my story can help others.

One of the challenges I face with writing about my addictions is what to tell and what not to tell. You must understand that dealing with an alcohol addiction remains a stigma for me. It is

Chapter 13   My Addiction: Coming Out of the Closet

easy enough to tell people that I quit drinking years ago and don't drink today. There are times when I want to tell all, be honest and transparent. However, when I go down that path I quickly retreat into my shell. The stories are embarrassing, they fill me with shame and guilt that brings about anxiety. And often when I reflect on this part of my journey, I have to stop my writing as I feel myself slipping into that dark place I don't want to be.

As I look back on that life, I don't like the view. I need to be intensely cognizant of the hurt I caused others. Although it was a battle for me, it was also a battle for others, particularly for my wife and my kids. So as much as I hope this provides some clarity for me, I hope it does the same for them.

As I have said before, anxiety is something I have lived with for as long as I can remember. Although there are times when my anxieties become less, they very easily surface again for no obvious reasons. Anxiety can be a debilitating problem.

Having a drink soothed the soul and eased mental anguish. Due to my perceived inabilities, it helped me fit in with people. It eased my social anxieties. It relaxed the body. It increased self-esteem. It provided for feelings of warmth for others. It increased motivation. It made me feel smarter, more creative.

It is a well-known fact that a drink provides relief, but the euphoria you experience only lasts twenty minutes. And then it takes up to two hours for the alcohol to leave your body. That means you drink for twenty minutes of relief only to feel even more miserable than you did before you had the drink. It becomes a vicious cycle.

To avoid the two hour "hangover," I would drink more. Till I drank too much. Then all bets were off. And when I drank too much, I experienced the exact opposite of what I was trying to accomplish. And trust me, there is a very fine line between the two. I would drink to solve one problem, but then needed to drink more to solve the problem that drinking created.

This created relational issues. As much as I drank to gain self esteem, to have more confidence, and to be better at relationships, the more that all suffered. The guilt and shame I felt when I saw the effects of my dependency issues on my wife and kids only drove me further into misery.

Being involved with alcohol is not something new to most of us, it seems to be part of life. Like most individuals, I too dabbled at an early age. I will never forget the day I stood at the beer vendor in our local town and tried to convince them that I was eighteen. The challenge was that the girl working that night was in the same grade as me, although a year older, and she knew all too well that I was not old enough to be buying beer. With enough persuasion she finally relented, and I was able to "pull' beer that night.

That beer really did nothing for me. As a matter of fact, I didn't like it. Over the years I would drink on occasion, but never to any great extent. Getting a buzz from a drink or two was enjoyable, but that was it. And then one day, I discovered the effects of hard liquor.

I clearly remember the day when I felt the magic, the release, the euphoria, and the satisfaction of booze. A few close friends and I went for a round of golf. Started innocently enough. We golfed. After the round we needed to wait for our wives to come join us for dinner. We waited in the bar, and I had a drink. I will never forget the effect that drink had on me. It was magical. The feeling coursing through my body was something I had never experienced before. It started with a warm, tingly feeling in my stomach. And then a profound sense of relaxation hit. It felt good, really good.

Perhaps that was the start. Initially it was not that difficult to control, and it certainly did not require a lot to get a slight buzz and then carry on with life. As the years progressed so did my intake of alcohol. It was interesting how the excuse to drink was readily available. Having a bad day? Drink. Having a good day? Drink. Having an in-between, mundane day? Drink.

Chapter 13   My Addiction: Coming Out of the Closet

As I became involved in agricultural politics, I quickly realized that I needed liquid courage. It felt like I had jumped into a vortex where I did not belong. I felt overwhelmed by what was expected of me and what I felt I could deliver. In my mind, those two were significantly separate from each other. I had never had self-confidence, my self-esteem was negligible, and courage was non-existent. I felt like a square peg trying to fit into a round hole.

That started a journey of drinking, sometimes in the morning, usually at night, and often in between. It provided the courage I needed, to be who I thought I needed to be. The following eight months remain a blur. I went from meeting to meeting, I travelled through Taiwan, South Korea, and Japan. And I was always waiting for meetings to be over so I could escape and go soothe my anxieties.

Although I was beginning to understand I had a problem, I had no idea of how to address it. At the time I was new to the world of alcohol dependency. While I was beginning to grapple with this, I heard someone tell a story about a golf pro who had turned to alcohol to cope with life. The storyteller used the words "the gentleman acquired a taste for alcohol" which ultimately ruined his marriage and his career. That hit me. It got me thinking. As much as I knew that I might have a problem, I still did not view it as an addiction because, in my mind, alcoholics were born with the illness, not something that built over time or was acquired.

Then came the time when it became clear to my wife that I was out of control. As much as I was trying to hide the amount I was drinking, the signs were there. I couldn't function as a father, finding it difficult to engage with my young kids. I was incapable of being the husband I needed to be. I was losing the ability to manage and work in the barn. I was taking risks in operating farm equipment and driving when I clearly shouldn't have.

Yes, I wanted to stop the train but had no clue how I could carry on without my liquid courage. There was a certain desperation in my thoughts. I knew I had to regain control of my life but was unable to fathom carrying on with my business, my work, and my relationships, without that crutch.

Fortunately, there was a feed salesman that I considered a friend, who was a recovering alcoholic. I asked him to come down for a chat and we visited. We exchanged stories. He listened and normalized and validated my fears of functioning without alcohol. He made it clear to me that I did have an addiction but in the same breath assured me there was hope and relief. He told me how much better I could be without alcohol. He gave me the encouragement that I needed to continue on a journey of sobriety.

When I first quit drinking, I was scared at the thought of having a drink. I knew what a slippery slope that had been—I wanted to avoid it at all costs. I knew it was a healthy fear, as it kept me vigilant. But over time, a complacency would set in, and I would let my guard down.

When we would go on winter vacations it was particularly difficult. For me it was a dream come true, to walk into a hotel room and booze was literally on tap, for free. I fooled myself into thinking that I could drink on vacation, but then quit once I got back home.

So I would sneak a drink or two. As it happens, I then needed to play the game. Drink but keep it hidden. Unfortunately, liquor has this ability to play with your mind and body. Finding the fine line between that feeling of euphoria and actually being somewhat inebriated is difficult. And obviously my personality would change. I would be more relaxed. I would talk more. That raised the suspicions of my wife who, one day, called me out on it, which led to a conversation.

The result of that conversation with her got me thinking of all the other times I had not been truthful with her regarding my addiction. It bothered me. I so much wanted to be honest with her, and yet I couldn't. What was it that kept me from that? In

Chapter 13 My Addiction: Coming Out of the Closet

our conversation that night, she suggested that she was trying to protect me from myself.

I suspect I was thinking more that she was trying to protect herself from me. If only I didn't drink, she would be fine. But if I could find any ray of truth to the situation, her way of thinking made sense. She fully understood that I had an addiction and that if she could only keep me from drinking, I wouldn't slip back into that dark world. She knew I was a better and happier person when I didn't drink.

But as much as it made sense, the drinking on that vacation was taking me down a road to where I didn't want to go. For the following four months I began a slow descent into what I knew could be trouble. I would find ways to imbibe at every opportunity, till I began to realize that I needed to stop before it went totally out of control.

As my wife alludes to, I had become quite proficient in hiding my drinking. But there were other factors at play as well. I needed to be done drinking at least two hours before my wife came home from work so as not to smell like a brewery. I also needed to quit drinking eight hours before bedtime, because I treasured a good sleep as that was my other defense against anxiety. When I would drink closer to bedtime, I would awake at night with increased anxiety. If I did not have any meetings, it was quite simple to meet my goals. A problem arose if I had meetings to go to because the window of opportunity became rather small.

It became obvious to me that I needed to quit while I still had enough of my wits about me. As they say, quitting is easy, it's not starting again that creates the problems. This is where it becomes difficult to quit on your own. There needs to be someone you can be accountable to. If no one knows you are drinking when you quit drinking, the only person who keeps you from drinking again is you. And trust me, the addicted you is not the best person to be accountable to.

It was the start of the golf season, and I knew that my golf would not be enjoyable if I carried on with my drinking. I knew that my wife and kids were starting to be suspicious. And I knew that this would start impacting my work if I did not deal with it.

I quit on a Friday. I went golfing Saturday morning. By the end of the golf game, I was already convincing myself that I should probably quit on a Monday rather than on a weekend. After the golf game, I was chatting with my wife and noticed she was wanting to say something but seemed hesitant. Finally, she just asked me quite simply when this latest episode with drinking would end.

Without hesitation, I blurted out, "yesterday." I felt a profound relief that she was asking this because I now knew I had that missing link. I would have to be accountable to her and my kids. Because of the relief I felt, I promptly sent my kids a text, saying that I had disappointed them, and that I would quit drinking.

They weren't particularly enthused about embracing that text. They felt that there was more needed. And, quite frankly, as I understood more about how my addiction had affected them, I knew I needed to have a conversation with them.

Because of the shame and guilt I felt for letting them down again, those conversations were not going to be easy. In the past, I had felt the anger and disappointment. And that became my primary reason for quitting. I assumed that this would be a replay of that, although I sensed from the approach my wife had taken, this might go differently.

It did go differently. They were open to discussing it. They were coming at this from a different perspective. They acknowledged that it had happened, that I had an illness, and it could happen again. All they could do was support me as best possible.

And here is the crux of my illness. My first thought was that they had given me the freedom to drink again. And perhaps that is, unintentionally, what it was. But as with other things in life, that freedom also gave me the freedom not to drink. In the past, I had quit but never become sober. I wasn't drinking, but I also was not dealing with what made me drink to begin with. There was an

Chapter 13 My Addiction: Coming Out of the Closet

understanding that I could not get sober for my wife, my kids, or my work. I could only quit when I decided I was done.

With their approach I could now freely address my addiction. That freedom gave me the opportunity to begin the healing process. As I found out, the physical component of not drinking was much easier to deal with than the emotional addiction. I needed to learn to face my emotions, to control my thoughts, to have awkward conversations. And most importantly, I needed to feel content with who I was, to feel comfortable in my own skin. I came to the understanding that addiction is giving up everything for one thing while recovering is giving up one thing for everything. That understanding gave me the ability to begin experiencing life as it was meant to be experienced.

I suppose because drinking was such a taboo in our home growing up, I still feel hesitant about telling people I don't drink. On the one hand, I don't want people to think I don't drink because of religious reasons. On the other hand, I don't necessarily need others to know I have an alcohol dependency issue. When we get together with others, I will often beg my wife to have a drink. She doesn't really care for alcohol, but in my mind if she has a drink, at least we won't come across as a sanctimonious, self-righteous couple.

A number of years ago, I was at the local arena watching a hockey game with a neighbour. A Lions Club member came around selling raffle tickets with the prize being a significant amount of liquor. My neighbour bought some tickets and after he was done the gentleman turned to leave. I stopped him and suggested that I would also like to buy some tickets, support the cause and all. He handed me the raffle book but made a comment about thinking I wouldn't buy tickets for booze because of who I was. That troubled me. I suppose having grown up in a community and having lived in that community for most of my life, there were those who had made certain assumptions of who I was by who I had been.

I will, on occasion, refer to my secret life, a life in a closet. I was a closet smoker because smoking was a sin and a big no-no in the home I grew up in. I was a closet drinker for years. Again, a big no-no for more than religious reasons. When it became more of a crutch, I did not want people to know how much I drank. I was in the closet with my mental health issues because of the stigma attached to it. I thought of it as a weakness.

Although the closet can be dark and lonely, being in there provided a sense of security. I viewed my alcohol dependency as a personal flaw, a vulnerability to be concealed. I feared that coming out would only exacerbate my already fragile state, not sure anyone would understand. And that could have the potential to deepen my anguish.

Essentially, what my family did was invite me out of the closet I was hiding in. That is worth repeating. My family invited me out of the closet! With that invitation, they were telling me that they understood my illness, and they were going to walk with me. With that invitation, I now had the ability to gain a sense of control over my life. Coming out of the closet, showing that vulnerability and being able to talk about it, came with a profound sense of relief. It was only in doing that that I was able to find a path forward. It was only by coming out, that I could address what was keeping me in the closet. I could now deal with the issues that were creating the addiction to begin with. And by understanding my mental health and the link to addiction, I was able to find the tools to keep me out of that closet.

Takeaway

Many of us have closets we hide in for a multitude of reasons. I feel I have been in and out of the closet numerous times in my life. If it wasn't smoking or drinking it was my mental illness. My financial issues kept me in there for quite some time. There are

Chapter 13 My Addiction: Coming Out of the Closet

things we live with or experience that we feel others wouldn't get or understand.

Being confined in a closet is not a pleasant thought. Use your imagination. Normally closets are dark and lonely places. Being in the closet has the potential to fill us with fear, shame, embarrassment, and guilt. Regardless of the issue we are loath to talk about, we visualize the response from others and the backlash it might create. We are consumed by our issue. We compare ourselves to others and wish we could trade places. Surely their life is better than ours. Their problems seem less than mine because nothing can be as bad as what I am experiencing. We differentiate between closets and make judgement on others, often thinking no one understands. No one else is hurting so why would they care.

When we see someone we care for hiding in their closet, we have a tendency to want to yank them out of there. We experience frustration at what we see. We think it should be easier for that person to want to be different, to come out of hiding. We want to dictate what we think they should do. Feeling that way does not indicate we care less. It means we don't have a clear understanding of many of the issues that keep folks in their closet. The problem with reacting this way is that the person in the closet may or may not step out. If they do, they do it for the sake of placating loved ones. Through that, they do not address the core issues of what was keeping them in their closet to begin with.

Being in a closet means a hard conversation needs to happen. Having that conversation has the potential to provide for relief and a better life. But how you ask? The word most often used to describe the ability to open up is vulnerability. To be vulnerable means to have the ability to let our guard down and be open and honest. That means being authentic and direct.

Perhaps, on the surface, embracing vulnerability seems straightforward. Unfortunately, being vulnerable can expose us to potential hurt. Some individuals lack understanding of the challenges that many people face. Consequently, when individuals attempt to open up, they face judgment and condemnation. I have heard comments like "I don't get it," "you need to get over it," "it's all in your head," or "it's a choice." I often wish those making such comments would engage in conversation with me, allowing me to explain the complexities of mental illness and addiction.

I have a deep appreciation for those who came and sat with me in the closet I was in. They were there not to be judgemental or provide some magical solutions, but rather to listen and to understand. That gave me the courage to step out and begin a new journey. But I also understand that there are those who do not have that type of support system. The challenge becomes to find someone or some group you can talk to, a safe place to be able to open up, be vulnerable and share the struggles that have kept you in the closet.

So come out of the closet. Free yourself from the darkness around you. Regardless of your reasons for being in the closet, let it be known. Don't be apologetic. Be proud of who you are and who you want to be. Find the support and help you need to overcome and to heal. Start living life the way it was meant to be lived. Be who you were meant to be. Coming out of the closet is a freeing, life-giving experience. So, open that door, come on out, and let's talk.

Chapter 14
Afraid of Living: But I Don't Want to Die

It's a hot summer day. We are camping with our young kids and some friends. To escape the heat and to take a break from the activities, I am sitting in the shade when I see a neighbour walk over. There was no usual greeting, he just simply stated a friend of mine had died. Although the news was shocking, what he said next stunned me. He tells me my friend had died by suicide. The shock was palpable. Although we had gone our separate ways after our teen years, I was now close friends with his parents. To try to fathom what my friend had been dealing with and ultimately done was difficult. To imagine the pain his family was feeling was beyond comprehension.

While I had never thought of myself as being suicidal, I did think about it. Professionals have since told me that it, in fact, means I was suicidal. As I said previously, the first few weeks after my diagnosis, I found myself thinking about the benefits of dying. That was largely driven by feelings of worthlessness, low self-esteem, feeling like a failure, and the fact that life insurance would be helpful for my wife and kids.

There is also what is known as passive suicidal ideation. That simply means that a person, at times, wishes they could die in their sleep, get hit by a car and die, or get sick and die. In some of my darker moments that certainly was the case. I had no intentions of hurting myself, but peacefully dying in my sleep seemed like a good option. It makes perfect sense to me when someone says, "I am not afraid of dying, I am afraid of living."

Suicide is no stranger to most of us. I remember, at the age of eleven, hearing about a thirteen-year-old neighbour boy dying by suicide. Initially, being quite young and not understanding suicide, I didn't fully grasp the impact at the time. But over the years, the tragedy struck me quite often, because I would drive by that farm and be reminded of what had happened.

My kids have lost friends to suicide. I lost friends to suicide. I suspect most of us know people who have died by suicide. Each and everyone is a tragedy. When I hear about a death by suicide I am filled with different emotions. First and foremost, there is profound sadness. That is often followed by anger, an intense frustration that this keeps happening. I always wonder, what could have been done to save those people. Even as I am writing this, I hear of a cousin who took his own life.

Some years ago, I received a call that shook me to the core. A person I was closely acquainted with had passed away by suicide. I had known her husband since childhood, and she, a loving wife and mother, had left us. The funeral was undoubtedly a somber occasion, especially given the circumstances. Yet, strangely enough, I left this one with a different set of emotions than I typically experience. Dare I say it left me feeling encouraged?

Too often people are loath to discuss suicide. Often times the cause of death is glossed over, perhaps in some attempt to run away from the tragedy. In this case, there was none of that. The family was open about what happened. Others that spoke, challenged us to be aware of mental health and the many that deal

Chapter 14 Afraid of Living: But I Don't Want to Die

with this insidious illness. We were reminded that the best way to support the family was through an acknowledgement and openness of her illness and her courageous fight.

During the service, one of her kids mentioned how, in the few short days since his mother's passing, they, as a family, had learnt a lot about mental illness. What caught my attention was when he suggested that had his mother suffered and ultimately died because of cancer, we would be talking about her courageous fight. We would talk about how brave she had been. He wanted everyone to know that his mother had fought a courageous battle. She had been brave. Her fight had been with a mental illness not a physical illness. But ultimately, she had lost.

That insight provided me with encouragement. Despite awareness campaigns regarding mental health illnesses there remains a stigma. People that suffer from mental illnesses often try to keep it a secret. We put on a mask hoping no one will know. We feel shame. And because of that we often do not seek the help we need. We must put aside the stigma. And for the people who suffer from mental health illnesses we have to understand that it is a fight. It takes courage. And when we come to that realization, we can take off our mask and show the people around us that we have the courage, and we need their support.

When I left that funeral, I experienced a number of conflicting emotions. I felt encouraged to understand that I along with many others were fighting courageous fights and not experiencing something to be ashamed and embarrassed about. I felt a tinge of envy that my friend's wife had escaped her pain. But I also felt an incredible fear, afraid that some morning I might wake up and just not be able to face the world any longer.

As with all suicides, this death was a tragedy beyond comprehension. It was a reminder for me to be aware of my own struggles and find better ways to deal with them. It was a reminder that there are many out there that face daily battles with their mental health. It was a reminder that more needs to be done. It was a reminder to seek understanding in spite of our own thoughts or beliefs. It was a challenge for all of us to be a support. A support to those who continue the courageous fight as well as a support to those who have lost a loved one to mental illness. It is also important to understand that, yes, the individual who died has escaped their pain, but the pain did not disappear. That pain was transferred to the ones left behind.

Maybe the reason why mental illness and suicide is still stigmatized is because it is too difficult for many of us to relate to mental pain and experience empathy for those who suffer from it. It is easy enough to "feel" someone's physical pain, because at some point in our lives we have experienced physical pain to some degree. To be able to empathize with and envision what people living with mental illness feel can be difficult. Truth be told, I often feel lost when describing what my experiences are, what my thoughts consist of, what my feelings are and the pain I often feel.

There is a further lesson here. Aside from ensuring that we reach out when we are experiencing mental illness, we must also make sure we check in with others. Quite often it is difficult to see when others are thinking about ending their life. In a suicide prevention workshop I took, we were taught that when we see signs that someone is struggling, we should not hesitate in asking outright whether they are considering killing themselves. Often we have the misconception that when we ask the question it will trigger a suicide attempt. Asking the question can open a dialogue about those feelings and how to best deal with them.

Initially that was difficult for me, it didn't feel right, it was awkward. I recall one evening a colleague phoning me about a client we had in farm debt mediation. She had just been talking to him and he had made veiled suggestions that the best thing was for him to die. She wasn't sure what to do.

So I called him, chatted a bit, and then I outright asked him if he was planning to kill himself. As it turns out, he was frustrated, feeling

Chapter 14   Afraid of Living: But I Don't Want to Die

helpless and hopeless about his situation. And as I had myself, he was thinking that death might be the best option. As we chatted more, I got the assurance from him that he was not planning on killing himself.

That was a learning experience for me. I understood better the importance of asking the question. I learned that asking the question provided an opportunity for the other party to talk and to share openly about their struggles. And I learned that at times it is the only way for someone to admit to their struggles, and through admitting it, be helped.

I have also learned that it is important to talk about the people I knew personally that died by suicide. It opens the door for others to talk about loved ones they lost. I know there can be uncomfortable feelings around that. It's almost like we avoid it because we think we will make others, particularly loved ones, sad by reminding them of someone who died. Trust me, you are not reminding them, they have not forgotten. What you are reminding them is that you remembered that the person lived and was loved.

Takeaway

Suicide and dealing with suicide have somewhat of a sordid history. Centuries ago, there were cultures that embraced suicide as an honorable act for certain situations. Others not so much. It got to the point where the Christian church condemned suicide. While its initial intent was to uphold the sanctity of life, it soon deteriorated into legalizing acts of cruelty against individuals struggling with suicidal thoughts, and their families. So if you attempted suicide and were unsuccessful, there was a good chance you could be arrested and be put to death. Talk about irony.

It is safe to say that there was a complete lack of understanding of mental illness and suicide. It is only in the last one hundred years or so that much of the condemnation has been replaced with an effort to better understand suicide. What is troublesome is that there are significantly different schools of thought and, as such, agreement about suicide and suicide prevention is unlikely. Because of that, the topic remains contentious and in many circles taboo.

Recently I was part of a conversation with two people, both quite religious, about mental illness. One was telling us about sometimes having a desire to die. Her chronic pain, her low self-esteem, and a complete feeling of hopelessness had pushed her to the brink. Quickly the conversation turned to the sinfulness of suicide. The guilt of even entertaining the thought was strong. I was saddened by what I heard. I wanted to say something, but I also knew that the topic and personal perceptions were rather sensitive.

I felt that should we be able to understand those suicidal thoughts, to realize that the urge to die was only a desire to escape pain, then and only then, could we make progress in dealing with the issues at hand. Being stuck on suicide being a sin, and in some circles an unpardonable sin, does nothing to help. It just creates feelings of guilt and shame which ultimately pushes us even closer to the edge. As that happens it becomes even more difficult to reach out for the critical help that is needed.

Some of these misguided thoughts on suicide hit home for me on another occasion. I was working with another conflict management specialist. At the end of our meeting, I mentioned to her that I was going to a funeral the following day for my kids' friend who had ended their life. Her comment, made in quite a judgemental tone, was that "suicide is such a selfish act." A feeling of rage enveloped me. I couldn't even respond and left quickly before I could say something I would regret.

In hindsight, I should have reacted differently. I could have explained to her why I felt her statement was not helpful. I have a notion that her response may have been defensive, or because of a lack of understanding, or a frustration due to her own life experiences. Perhaps for her to tag suicide as selfish was easier than trying to understand why someone would choose to die. But to suggest that

Chapter 14 Afraid of Living: But I Don't Want to Die

taking your own life is selfish does nothing but insult the deceased and shows an incredible lack of understanding of mental illness.

After that brief exchange, I felt it important to look into the whole "suicide is a selfish act" to make sure that the next time this happened, I could be more prepared to respond. One piece I read mentioned people jumping from the twin towers during the horrors of 9/11. The suggestion was that the people had not had a desire to die, but were jumping to escape the pain from the intense fire they were in. That made sense to me. When we feel physical pain, we react. And most times we don't take the time to figure out what the consequences of our reaction will be. We should never confuse ending our mental pain with ending our life.

Because of the different thoughts and beliefs about suicide, there remains a general lack of understanding. Furthermore, some of the beliefs bring on certain biases that only get in the way of helping those with mental illness and thoughts of killing themselves.

I have also sometimes said that I am not afraid of dying, I am afraid of living. It is important to note that does not mean I wanted to die. It means that I was desperately looking for solutions to get me away from those thoughts of dying.

As much as the conversation might be uncomfortable, as much as we may have certain biases and as much as the subject might be taboo, we need to get past that. We need to find ways to understand. We need to find ways to help. We need to make sure that our family members, our friends, our neighbours and even strangers can feel comfortable in broaching the subject. We need to ensure that we are comfortable asking the question. It is only then that we can become proactive in saving lives, helping those that are hurting and those who are afraid of living but don't want to die.

If you or someone you know is struggling and contemplating suicide, avail yourself of the resources available in most jurisdictions. Canada has a national suicide line. You can call or text **988**. More information can be found at https://talksuicide.ca/.

Chapter 15
Don't Suffer in Silence: Building a Bridge

I force myself to go to the barns. It is two days after I witnessed my brother's motorbike accident. He is lying in a coma in the hospital and all the farm work has been thrust on my shoulders. The world is a dark place for me. The events of the last few days have pushed me to the abyss. As I walk towards the barn, my neighbour shows up. He clearly senses that I am not in a good place. He asks me how I am doing. And for some strange reason I start talking. I verbalize the myriad of thoughts racing through my head. He sits and listens; he normalizes and validates my thoughts. He doesn't provide any magical solutions but the listening ear he gave me that morning was just what I needed.

I have a notion that with the ongoing and increasing awareness around mental health, there are those that would like to talk about it but still struggle due to the stigma, mired in a secret life hiding in a closet. Why? Because we are filled with guilt, because we feel shame, because our self-esteem cannot take another blow. So, we keep it a secret. We hope to wake up tomorrow and have the issue resolved.

Chapter 15 Don't Suffer in Silence: Building a Bridge

We are also convinced that no one will believe us. I come from a generation where it was easier to ignore or deny issues. That meant that people with mental health issues, didn't. Where people with financial struggles, didn't. Where people with relational issues, didn't. Clearly any struggles we had were because we did not work hard enough, or we did not pray enough, or our faith was not strong enough. We were good at hiding stuff. And often when a person showed vulnerability and dared to talk about their struggles, they were told to "get over it."

Over the years I have been privileged in having friends that I could share with. I have come to a full understanding of the benefits of being able to talk about my anxiety and depression. I often tell people that verbalizing the ruminations and wild thoughts racing through my head brings them out into the open. And through that I get to better understand what is real and what is perceived. That makes dealing with it much easier. But I also came to realize that there are times when I needed professional help.

The challenge I ran into was that I had co-occurring disorders. Although significant change has happened, back in the day addictions and mental illness were separated and not harmonized. So when seeking help it was an either/or situation. That meant that when you ended up in the system you had to deal with them separately. Thankfully that has changed whereby the caregiver now can address the disorders simultaneously.

As part of my initial diagnosis, my family doctor referred me to a psychiatrist. As we discussed my anxiety and depression, he asked whether there had been any mental illness in my family. I acknowledged that there had been. We talked about any symptoms I might have had previously, including during my teen years. I was open about the struggles I was having on the farm, particularly the ongoing financial issues and suggested to him that selling the farm could be a benefit for my mental wellness. I will never forget that he suggested strongly that I would be dealing with anxiety and depression for the rest of my life. He did not make it sound hopeless, rather just gave me a heads-up that selling the farm might not be the only answer. And it wasn't.

Shortly after my neighbour checked in on me, my wife and I were discussing my mental health situation and wondering what to do. We chatted about the effect medication had on my life, work, and relationships. We decided that instead of going on meds, I should try talk therapy. Furthermore, we agreed that I should start with a psychologist. I made the appointment and went for what I expected to be the first of several sessions.

In the initial appointment, I told the psychologist my story. I told him about the ongoing stressors of farming. I related how the financial pressure had brought me down. I told him that my brother and I had agreed that we needed to sell the farm. He was taken aback that we would consider selling the family farm. He asked how we could justify that. And when my hour with him was up, he told me to go back on meds because I couldn't afford him.

I was devastated. It rattled me. Did that mean I was a hopeless case? Was talk therapy not supposed to help? But we didn't give up. We decided I should try a community mental health worker. But after two appointments with her, she basically said that as long as I owned the farm I would be dealing with anxiety and depression and that, perhaps, medication would be best.

Although I appreciated her honesty, I was significantly discouraged. I went back to my doctor and asked for an antidepressant prescription. I thought that was the only hope left. I stayed on those till well after the farm was sold and then went off them because of numerous side effects I was experiencing.

Over the years I have had to revisit the various resources that are available for those with mental illness. I, at times, compare myself with my car. It needs regular maintenance. Sometimes the check engine light comes on. Unfortunately, I am not the best with car maintenance. I am always concerned that anything small will

Chapter 15   Don't Suffer in Silence: Building a Bridge

turn into something major as soon as I go to the garage. So too, I am with my mental health.

But there are times when I say enough is enough and do try things. At one point, I was sharing with a colleague about being mentally weary, life just not feeling that great. I suppose with all that was going on with my mental health, the thought of reaching out to another professional was overwhelming me. She encouraged me to make that appointment, so I did. It was interesting how just the step of making another appointment already provided some relief.

The appointment was with a psychologist who was quite familiar with my story and the work I do. He co-facilitated the men and depression workshops with me, so he had heard my story. Leading up to the appointment, I spent considerable time and effort in analyzing what I thought might be going on inside my brain. I read material on mindfulness. I did an inventory of what was creating my blue feelings. I made excuses. It was close to Christmas, a time of year I typically struggle. I dreaded the thought of going back on medication.

I thought I had done it all and expressed a frustration to the psychologist that nothing seemed to work. He suggested to me that it sounded like my emotional gas tank had run dry. He went on to tell me that the work I do, dealing with people in crisis, was having a negative impact on my own emotional state. He said that even if I didn't recognize it, negative energy could have that effect. He asked me when the last time was that I had done something for myself. He asked me what type of activities I enjoyed. Facetiously, I suggested to him that I needed him to contact my wife and suggest to her that I needed to go south for the next two months to golf. I left that appointment with a great deal of relief. Obviously, I had over complicated the issues. Clearly I needed to be aware of when my emotional gas tank was running low and then be proactive in filling it.

149

But as I came to understand, mental health can be like a roller coaster. As much as it might improve it can also deteriorate, so when I found myself slipping towards the abyss, I would seek further help.

Making appointments can be challenging. Just finding a professional to talk to can be so frustrating that people often give up before they have started. Wait times can be atrocious. When my daughter was experiencing prenatal anxiety, the wait time to see a professional was seven months. She had been told that the prenatal anxiety could clear up or, at minimum, ease after three months. Having to wait seven months was not helpful. All her family doctor did was offer to pray for her.

To complicate matters further, I would need a referral from my doctor to get in to see a psychologist. I went to see my doctor, who was more than willing to provide the referral. But he also acknowledged that the wait time would be considerable, so he suggested I see a therapist in their clinic. I was ready to try anything so agreed to that.

I went through the typical initial conversation with the therapist. I gave her my life history, talked about my farming escapades, talked about the work I do and about the training I had in conflict and stress management. She told me that we could cover things like mindfulness and cognitive behavioural therapy. I was quick to tell her that I had learned all those theories and concepts in my training and that they were not helpful. I didn't admit to her that I lacked the patience to utilize some of those tools.

Exasperated, she finally asked me how she could help me. I suggested to her that, first and foremost, I needed to take control of my mind, my stinking thinking as it were. She responded rather quickly that she had an easy trick for that. Her answer almost discouraged me. I had heard of so many "easy tricks" in the past which just never seemed to work for me. I knew I was guilty of giving up too easily. And yet, I was ready to try almost anything.

Chapter 15 Don't Suffer in Silence: Building a Bridge

She asked me to close my eyes and think of something, anything. She then said I should think about that till she clapped her hands, and then I was to drop my tongue. Sounds weird, I know, but hear me out. We did that once. She asked me what I noticed. Quite frankly, I wasn't sure what I was supposed to notice. So we did it again. And after I had dropped my tongue and opened my eyes, I got it. When I dropped my tongue, my mind went clear. No longer was I thinking about what I had been thinking about. It worked. (More on this in Chapter 16.)

When I left that appointment, I was not entirely sold on the concept. However, I thought I would try it. I found out rather quickly that it does work. But I was still not ready to start sharing that too widely. For the next while when I chatted with friends and family, I would mention the tongue trick. Invariably they would come back to me and let me know it worked.

At the outset, I mentioned that when dealing with co-occurring disorders, finding the right help can be a struggle. As I was dealing with my anxiety and depression, the urge to drink did not go away. The caregivers I had seen previously, aside from the psychologist mentioned earlier, had all tried to fix my mental health but something was still missing.

Clearly there was a connection between my mental illness and my addictions issues. With my experience finding someone to talk to, I was at wits' end. My wife suggested a naturopath. I was somewhat less than enthused about that appointment. I was convinced that I would come home with a bag of supplements and a diet of everything I have refused to eat in the past. But I thought I owed it to my wife and children to find a way to be healthier.

The appointment was scheduled for one and a half hours and turned out to be one of the most helpful appointments I have ever experienced. Finally, someone who explored various parts of my past and was able to connect many dots for me. Someone who addressed both mental health and dependency issues. It felt like therapy, a therapy that had promise. My wife was quite surprised to see me come home from that appointment with a smile on my face.

As I suggested earlier, it is not easy describing mental illness. When the naturopath asked me how my depression felt, I found it hard to explain. I wondered whether it was like a constant cloud hanging over me but knew that was not accurate. She finally put it into words for me. She asked whether the sun was shining but I was just not feeling the warmth. That described exactly what I was feeling.

When I talked to her about my inability to feel love she explained about dopamine and that what I was expressing fit with a lack of that particular chemical. She went on to explain that alcohol provides fuel for dopamine and that is why when I had a drink or two, I felt love and an enthusiasm for relationships.

My wife and I had wondered and talked about what triggered my desire to drink. It has always been difficult for me to pinpoint certain triggers. The doctor helped me understand why something like a vacation would make me want to drink. She explained that when I was outside my comfort zone, in this case being away from home, my brain was telling me to drink. I realized how my imposter syndrome had been, and continued to be, a trigger. I wanted so badly to feel at peace and capable, I turned to alcohol because it provided a sense of comfort and control. It literally made me feel comfortable in my own skin.

She helped me understand that because of a lack of dopamine I was looking outward for relief, looking to forget, for relief from pain, a sense of calmness, and a desire to escape my own mind, to simply not be myself for a few hours.

She further explained that the reason I felt so much anger, often about false narratives conjured up in my mind, the reason I felt I couldn't love, and the anxious moments often experienced in the mornings, was because of low dopamine levels.

Chapter 15 Don't Suffer in Silence: Building a Bridge

Furthermore, she explained why antidepressants had not been particularly effective for me. Antidepressants help for an imbalance with serotonin, another chemical prevalent in our brains. She wondered whether my focus should be directed at my dopamine rather than serotonin.

For some time, I had often described my alcohol disorder as a mental/emotional addiction rather than a physical addiction. I had talked to various people about that through the years and had always been met with skepticism. The doctor was in full agreement with my assessment. She did suggest however, that it starts as a mental addiction but as the drinking carries on it does become physical.

As the doctor listened and explored with me my journey of depression, anxiety and addictions, she showed an amazing insightfulness. What I found intriguing about the dopamine situation was twofold. Alcohol causes the brain's reward system to release the motivational chemical dopamine. But over time, chronic drinking actually depletes the amount of dopamine in your brain, causing you to crave more alcohol and laying the groundwork for an alcohol addiction.

Secondly, low dopamine levels inhibit one's ability to engage in meaningful relationships. For example, mornings would find me being angry. Not for any reason other than my brain would conjure up these thoughts, most of them not real, and create intense levels of anger. I found it difficult to join my wife for morning coffee. Hugging anyone was out of the question. I had a difficult time accepting myself and finding the motivation to do things I enjoyed, even something as enjoyable as golf.

What a sense of relief I felt on my journey home that afternoon. Not only had someone connected dots for me, but the potential fix also seemed simple enough. I was avoiding, as best I could, going back on meds but because it was a naturopath I was seeing, I was convinced I would need to change my diet, which I was less than

153

enthused about. It turned out I didn't need to concern myself with that. I didn't need to change my diet or go on meds. All I needed to do was increase my protein intake, particularly in the mornings. That would help my brain produce the dopamine I needed.

Figuring out mental health can be a complicated and frustrating experience. What works for one may not work for someone else. It would be so much simpler if it could be done with X-rays, MRIs or even blood tests. What I learned is to never give up. Sometimes it means seeking a second, third, or even fourth opinion.

There are times I wonder how tired people must be about hearing this ongoing issue of mental health and "talking about it." I get really tired of it myself, to the point of getting quite angry. Why the hell can't we just be happy? Why do we need to continuously remind people to talk? And then I sit back, look at my own life, look at my own struggles, and I understand. I get it. What has helped me has helped others as well. The first step in healing is talking about it.

Over the years I have talked on many occasions. I have come to the realization that there are so many folks out there that listen. So many that do understand. So many that welcome the opportunity to help. Like the neighbour who took the time to ask when I was in my darkest moment. Or the friend who listened without judgement. A wife and partner who never gave up on me. My kids who did care even when I thought I was protecting them from the demons of my inner self. And the countless people who approached me when they realized that I too was experiencing what they had felt for years. And the professionals out there who help folks like me on a daily basis.

Although many people experience mental health issues there are those who do not. For those people, I can only throw out one challenge. Take the time to listen. The beauty of that is you don't need to provide any answers. All you need to do is show some interest, be curious, normalize, validate, and understand in

Chapter 15   Don't Suffer in Silence: Building a Bridge

whatever way you can. That is all many of us need. That is all we ask for. And the more we are able to talk, the more we can be on that road to recovery. A road filled with a true peace and contentment. A road that can provide for a better tomorrow.

There is a certain camaraderie out there. As long as we hide behind a façade of happiness, of contentment, of peace, we never find it. But it is there. And it is so helpful. Thank you to all those that have taken the time to listen to me in the past. Thank you to all who have encouraged without judgement. Thank you to all those who stuck with me even when I stumbled and fell. Thank you to all who continue to care. You have no idea how helpful you have been in my journey. A journey that continues and will continue to the day I die.

Takeaway

Some time ago, one of my kids said to one of their siblings, "get over it." In the background I heard someone else say, "build a bridge." Excuse me. Build a bridge? Sure, they said, when you are told to get over it, what do you need? You need a bridge. That simple.

That got me thinking of the mental health journey so many of us are on. At times it feels like we have walked into a river with a swift and turbulent current. As you start across the river the water gets deeper. Mud is sucking at your feet. The current is throwing you off balance. An alligator or two are nipping at your heels. The water gets colder. Then when the water gets too deep for walking you start swimming. The current takes you downstream and you end up in places you had not wanted to go. In a worst-case scenario, you can drown.

Now picture crossing that same river on a bridge. You stay dry. You stay on course. You stay safe. Now you can observe the river from above. There are no threats to life or limb. And once that bridge has been built it can be used time and time again.

Having the ability to talk about our mental health struggles, seeking help from professionals or any other means of opening up and talking about it is the best way to build that bridge. When we show vulnerability and we seek that support, we get the tools and resources needed to build that bridge. Sure, having to build a bridge will take some time and some effort. But when it is built it becomes a way to circumvent a lot of problems.

There is another side to this. Very often we find it difficult to respond to friends or family members who are hurting. Perhaps it is because we feel that to respond means we take responsibility for their problems. Maybe we are unsure of what to say. Trust me. I know from experience that people experiencing mental pain wish they were not. They would like to be part of a normal world, whatever that means. By simply being there, normalizing and validating as you listen, you are in fact helping to build a bridge for them.

The tools and resources are available. Be proactive in finding those tools and resources that will work for you. The best part of this is you don't need to do this on your own. Friends, family, neighbours, and professionals are all prepared to be on the "construction" crew. They are your supports. Let's build more bridges and together "get over it." Don't suffer in silence.

CHAPTER 16
What Works for Me: Taming the Beast

I wake up early in the morning. Anxiety hits like a ton of bricks. Any sound I hear makes my nerve endings vibrate, coursing through my hands and echoing in my head. An impatience, a restlessness, wraps around me, making the simple act of leaving my bed a scary thought. It leaves me mystified. When I went to bed last night, this day had so much promise. Now I am left with empty feelings of hopelessness. The temptation is there to simply cover my head with the blanket and stay right there. But I know that won't help. What I do know is that within an hour of getting up, things will be better. They usually are.

Understanding Mental Illness

As you are aware by now, gaining an understanding of my mental health, or lack thereof, has been an integral part of my journey. With all the appointments I have had with professionals, the ones where someone could connect dots for me were the most helpful. Not that they fixed me, but with the understanding came ways of making my life better.

There are times I will be hard on myself because of my anxiety and depression. I see others who have dealt with significant life-altering trauma who are struggling. I tell myself that based on their experiences; I should be better. I needed to understand that trauma comes in a variety of forms. As much as we view sexual, physical, or emotional abuse as trauma, trauma can also involve unhealthy relationships, financial distress, or a host of other things.

I am uncomfortable when others tell me that regardless of what they are experiencing, someone else has it worse. All that does is minimize your own issues and suggests your struggles are insignificant. That leads to hiding, refusing to cry out, and not wanting to burden those close to us. Others may well have it worse, but we have to recognize our experiences as being what they are and seek out ways of improving our mental health. It is not a competitive game.

I needed to better understand the intricacy of my brain and how different chemicals needed to be in balance for my mental health to thrive. Through that understanding, I am able to utilize various methods that help. Through that understanding I can be proactive in bringing more balance to my mental health.

Being Aware

I have to recognize when life begins to overwhelm. I know that my tolerance for stress is much diminished from what it once was. Something as simple as my wife wanting to discuss financial matters increases my anxiety, similar to the anxiety I felt when dealing with our farm finances. When I get too wrapped up in my work, I find myself easily becoming discouraged. I find loud noises increase my heart rate and pressure builds in my head.

I once asked a friend what had caused him to become depressed. His answer has stuck with me. He said his depression came when he was asked to give and he had nothing left to give.

Chapter 16 What Works for Me: Taming the Beast

That reminded me of the psychologist suggesting my emotional gas tank was empty.

The body goes through an interesting process when a person is in a state of high anxiety. It starts in the brain with the amygdala, which I call the radar centre. When it detects potential danger it sends a distress signal to the hypothalamus which activates the sympathetic nervous system which sends signals to the adrenal glands which in turn pumps adrenaline into the bloodstream. This elevates the body's cortisol levels, and when that happens too often, it can disrupt many of your body's processes and increases the risk of, you guessed it, anxiety and depression. I suspect we have all experienced that. You know that feeling you get when you're travelling down the highway, see a police car, check your speedometer, and realize you are speeding? At least for me, that always gives me an adrenaline rush. Still not sure if that's because of seeing the police or whether that's because I know what the reaction from my wife will be if I come home with a speeding ticket.

My amygdala, or radar centre, seems to be hypervigilant. Under normal circumstances, it should warn me of danger. But no, unexpected noises, and they don't have to be particularly loud, will set off the process. It senses danger when I get up in front of people to talk. Even with my everyday work, something as simple as checking emails or voice messages sets off the amygdala, shooting adrenaline into my system, increasing waves of anxiety. Since childhood I have had the shakes. My father always told me I would never be a surgeon. With elevated anxiety, those shakes become even worse.

So the first hour or two in the day, brings about increased anxiety. Normally that anxiety eases and I can carry on with the day. In the evenings I feel invigorated, ready to conquer the world. And then I am reminded that today was the day I was so worried about in the morning. And it turned out good.

Over the years, through counselling training, talking with others and my own experiences, I have found various tools that help me in maintaining a certain level of mental wellness. That helps me in managing my mental health. Just keep in mind, what works for me, may not work for everyone. At times it's a matter of trial and error.

Negative Self Talk

I struggle with negative thought patterns and when left unfettered they cause even more negativity in my life. I find it rather interesting how those thoughts can conjure up stories—stories that are completely fabricated.

I often find my thoughts in a feedback loop. And because I know better than to allow those thoughts, I start bemoaning the fact that I have these negative thoughts and that I am such an idiot for thinking them and such a loser for thinking that I am an idiot and because I am an idiot it is no wonder I am useless at this thing called life. Notice how quickly I can get myself in trouble?

I will at times refer to an imaginary parrot I have on my shoulder. We all know that a parrot is the only animal that can be taught to talk. But it will only repeat what it hears. Most of us are our own worst critic. So when I berate myself, call myself an idiot, the parrot repeats that. To change that narrative, I must feed the parrot positive words. I have to use the same compassion with myself that I would use with others.

Positive Thinking

I have also had to learn to change my thinking. It is virtually impossible to push negative or anxiety-inducing thoughts out of your brain. You can't tell the brain not to do something. Allow me to use golfing as an example. When you need to hit a ball over the water and all you are thinking is, don't hit it in the water, that becomes your focus. And, you guessed it, the chances are good

Chapter 16 What Works for Me: Taming the Beast

you will hit it in the water. If you focus on the obstacles, all you will see is the obstacles. But if you focus on your goal, it becomes easier to hit your target.

When I give presentations to different groups, I often engage them in a thought exercise. I instruct them to imagine themselves in Churchill, watching polar bears. The vast tundra stretches before them, and they're engrossed in observing these majestic creatures. However, in the next moment, I ask them to picture a massive bear suddenly rearing up on its hind legs, poised to attack. Then I ask that they close their eyes and try not to think about this threatening bear. It's a curious phenomenon—the mere act of attempting not to think about the bear becomes incredibly challenging because our brains are wired to persistently bring it to the forefront of our thoughts.

However, what really works is to introduce good, healthy thoughts to your brain. So I tell the group to again close their eyes but now present a different scenario to them. I tell them to envision they are sitting beside a bubbling brook, the sun warming their backs, hearing the sound of the breeze in the leaves and birds chirping in the trees. That is much easier to do than trying to ignore the bear. It changes your perspective. Although I should add, with one group we went through this exercise and when I asked for comments after, one gentleman said it worked well, he had been relaxing by the brook when suddenly the polar bear came charging through the trees. Now that is someone I can relate to.

What I did years ago, and it still works today, is find my happy place. I am an avid golfer so when I wake up at night, worrying about something or feeling incredibly anxious, I will pick a golf course and start playing it in my mind. Usually I only play a few holes and I drift back to sleep. It takes effort to concentrate on golf and on occasion something will distract me and off I go into the world of anxiety. Then I have to bring myself back.

Drop Your Tongue

I mentioned previously about the therapist who taught me the trick of dropping my tongue. She explained to me that research has shown that when you drop your tongue it is virtually impossible to think clearly about anything specifically for any length of time. It brings you back to the present. Next time you are deep in thought about an issue take note of where your tongue is. You will find it is firmly placed against the roof of your mouth.

Sometime ago I awoke at night and found my thoughts racing from one thing to another. That was unusual, because normally I would be fixated on a certain topic that would be anxiety inducing. I thought about the tongue trick, checked my tongue and found it was not up against the top of my mouth. That made me wonder whether the tongue trick could work in reverse. I knew that if I could focus on golf, my mind would relax, and I might be able to sleep again. So I planted my tongue firmly against the roof of my mouth and started playing the first hole at my golf course. Much to my relief, I found that worked as well.

Boosting My Dopamine

I continue with having protein first thing in the morning. Nothing exotic, just a simple glass of milk mixed with protein powder. That has literally changed my life. Without question it has helped in the natural production of dopamine. My desire to drink is greatly diminished. Mornings, generally, are much better. My feelings for others have greatly improved. My self-esteem is better.

It's another one of those things that sounded suspicious to me at the outset. Shortly after that appointment, still not entirely convinced about dopamine being the problem, my wife and I watched a show that involved hospitals and doctors. I normally watch these types of shows for entertainment but do wonder about whether

Chapter 16 What Works for Me: Taming the Beast

any of it is based on real facts. In the episode we were watching, a woman was experiencing certain issues that required brain surgery. She was forewarned that the surgery could well impact her brain's ability to produce dopamine and what that might look like. When I heard those words, I took note. After her surgery, her son comes and gives her a hug. She returns the hug and says "I love you." As the boy leaves the room, she looks at her doctor and asked; "Do you think he felt that I really didn't mean it?" Needless to say, that hit home with me.

Learning to Say No

I have learned that I need to limit my exposure to things that stress me out. Following anything or anyone on social media these days provides a plethora of thoughts, ideas, and beliefs. Many of those do nothing for my mental health. I used to watch a lot of news but have had to quit that. There seems to be so many negative events in the world that seeing that brings on more anxiety.

I have this thing called a Fitbit. At first, I thought it would be a great idea to track my exercise, check on my heartbeat, see how many calories I am burning and remind me EVERY HOUR ON THE HOUR that I need to walk. It will vibrate and when I check, it tells me to "feed it." It's a constant reminder to do better. It seems that I never measure up, so I turned off the notifications. I did not want to be reminded.

That is what I have found works best. Turn off notifications with the news, Facebook, X (formerly Twitter) and all other sources that are feeding us. I know, if you don't keep up you are uninformed and if you do keep up, you are misinformed. I have found that being uninformed is much healthier for me.

Human Connection

Human connection is incredibly important for my mental health. But, as an introvert, that comes with some challenges. When I am struggling, I have a tendency to withdraw or isolate myself. I bottle up things. I may feel shame. My pride takes a hit. My self-esteem slips even lower. I begin to believe that I am the only one having these experiences. And then I become captive in my own world, unable to see beyond my own pain.

As I stated earlier, it has been said that we are the loneliest society in history. We have the ability to connect in so many ways, but are we really connecting? Connection is a core human need. It is having shared experience, relatable feelings and similar ideas. The stress prevalent in the world today, only exacerbated by things like Covid, creates a damaged ability to connect with others because we isolate ourselves and try to hide.

I have found that when I build on relationships, when I share with others, I gain the freedom that I desperately strive for. That helps me think outside the box. I discover a world I had forgotten existed. And with that comes an improvement in my mental health.

After two and a half years of Covid, we were invited for a weekend reunion at our friends' place. It included three families that used to camp annually when our kids were young. Now the kids are all grown up and there are grandkids involved. For three days I enjoyed the company of my friends. It was relaxing to sit, visit, watch our kids reconnect, and watch our grandkids playing. That weekend reiterated for me what human connection can do for my mental health.

Shortly after that weekend, my daughter sent the family a text saying they had booked a campsite if anyone wanted to join them. I felt some guilt at that, as my wife had been pushing for years that we should go camping again. I thought that I needed to accommodate her wishes and so made arrangements to borrow a camper. It turns out that camping seems to be good for my mental health too. When I mentioned that to my wife, she said how noticeable that had been.

Treating My Body Well

Use a treadmill they said. It will help I was told. Ugh. Apparently, I now need to exercise for three reasons. First, it helps my lungs. As I have stated earlier, I have COPD. The doctor says to keep it at bay, I need to exercise my lungs. Secondly, I have always struggled with my weight. Winters are particularly bad for that because of inactivity. And last, and maybe most important, exercise releases endorphins which help with anxiety and depression.

And I know full well that exercise helps me for all of the above reasons. Normally after summer activities end and the golf season is over, I am quite diligent in using the treadmill. Recently, as I have done in the past, at the start of November I had commenced my exercise routine. For some reason it did not have the typical result. My mental health was not improving. There were a number of personal issues that were creating anxiety. Then at the beginning of December, a difficult mediation file pushed my anxiety to levels I had not experienced in a number of years. It was discouraging. But I needed to push through that. As much as the willpower was lacking, I knew that exercise helps, so kept at it.

There are other aspects of our physical bodies that need care. It is intriguing to learn about the connection between our physical health and our mental health. When I suggested to my naturopath that I was concerned about my serotonin being out of balance and I was contemplating going back on antidepressants, she suggested that there was a more natural way of getting similar benefits to what medication would give me. Through a series of blood tests, she determined there were certain elements out of balance in my body. She put me on a regiment of supplements which has had a significantly positive effect on my mental health and, by extension, my physical health as well. Recently my daughter asked me how that was working. I suggested she ask her mother who quickly said it felt like she was now experiencing her fifth husband, even better than number four. I am taking that as a good thing.

And never underestimate sleep. I know many folks that struggle with getting a good night's sleep. I am incredibly grateful that I can sleep as well as I do. As a matter of fact, I treasure my sleep. Quite often it feels like my brain is pushing me to go to sleep. I am convinced that it knows that when I sleep, it can quiet down and the mind and body can relax. But the brain does not always cooperate either. There are times when I do go to bed and then the brain goes "wait a minute" and sends my thoughts spiralling. Then I have to revert back to finding my happy place.

Jump-start the Day

As a self-employed person working out of a home office, I sometimes find it difficult to focus on the work I need to get done. If I have a meeting to go to it is simple. You get up, get ready, and go. The pandemic changed that. Most of my work was being done virtually. That meant seldom leaving my office. If I didn't have a specific appointment, it was quite easy to let my anxiety-ridden mind get distracted by anything but work that should be done. It became far too easy to procrastinate. And the more I procrastinated, the harder it became to do what needed to be done.

I learned that having a routine was important. That often meant forcing myself to make that phone call, to finish up that paperwork that needed to be done, to prepare for the next meeting, or even to write more. It was interesting how quickly my mental health changed when I did that. I went from procrastinating to feeling invigorated. I went from feelings of hopelessness to feelings of hope and happiness.

Chapter 16   What Works for Me: Taming the Beast

Laughter is a Good Medicine

I need to learn to laugh more. As I said previously, laughter can be a powerful antidote for stress and pain. Based on research, nothing works faster to bring your emotions back into balance than a good laugh. My friend from the Manitoba Pork days and I have this interesting way of finding things to laugh about. Back in the days when we would travel with other folks, they were often mystified because the two of us would be busting a gut laughing, and they would have no idea why. Not sure we always did either. Even now when we get together as couples, one of us will say something that makes the other person laugh, and in no time both of us are laughing, and our wives can only look and wonder why. And each time that happens, my mental health improves.

Surviving Tough Times

I find fall and early winter to be particularly distressing for me. As the days get shorter, the weather turns colder, and as snow flies, I feel my anxiety increasing. And with that comes an increase of depression. Quite often, during this time of year, I wonder about going back on medication.

Suffice it to say I have often questioned why my ancestors got off the train in Manitoba. Surely they could have found a place that didn't experience the harsh winters, a time of year when days are shorter and nights longer. Sorry, I digress. What I do to help with the darkness and lack of sun, is use a SAD (seasonal affective disorder) lamp or, as it is often called, a "happy light."

The light box emits light that replicates sunlight, addressing the absence of natural light during the darker winter months. Insufficient exposure to light in this season can disrupt your circadian rhythm, potentially resulting in decreased energy, feelings of worthlessness, and difficulty concentrating. It is believed that this specific light exposure may induce a chemical change in the brain, uplifting mood, and alleviating other symptoms associated with SAD.

As December turns to January followed by February there comes a sign of better things to come. Days are getting longer. The normal high daytime temperature begins to go up. You know there is hope. Summer brings an improvement to my mental health for a variety of reasons. I love to golf, and as luck would have it, I live on a golf course. So I take full advantage of that. Hitting the links as the sun rises, getting together with friends and hitting some balls is a definite mood enhancer. It's a great way to start the day. And with our warm summer temperatures, other activities are much more conducive to a happier life. The natural vitamin D is just a bonus.

The Power of Music

Never underestimate the incredible power of music, whether you're an avid listener or a musician. I discovered my love for playing the guitar at a young age, and soon after, I taught myself to play the harmonica. To my surprise, I even managed to play them together, creating a unique musical experience. While these instruments often find themselves gathering dust in my closet, there are those special moments when I take them out and play. Every time I do, I find that my mood experiences a remarkable improvement.

But music's influence extends far beyond playing it. Simply listening to music has the ability to soothe the soul and elevate one's mood. In my earlier years, I spent a significant amount of time driving along the highways and byways. During these journeys, my mind would often wander into less than helpful, or even unhealthy, territories. However, the moment I turned on the radio and tuned into some good music, my trips instantly transformed into more enjoyable experiences.

Chapter 16 What Works for Me: Taming the Beast

During Covid, after having worked in isolation for some time, I felt myself sliding down that slippery slope of misery. Aside from the isolation, news from around the world wasn't good on a number of fronts. Finally, in desperation, I hopped in my car and went for a drive. No destination, just wanting to get out, to get away.

As I drove aimlessly, listening to music, the Beatles' song "Let It Be" came on. I found my spirits rising as I sang along. Those three words, "let it be," gave me comfort. They helped me come back to the present, breathe deeply, and take control of my thoughts. I got home and felt renewed energy to carry on with life.

Using My Supports

I am keenly aware of the importance of relationships in maintaining my mental wellness. First and foremost, I know I would not have survived my journey had it not been for my wife and kids. When I find myself getting weary and feel like giving up on my walk through the labyrinth, I often find my wife, my kids, their partners and my grandkids ready to encourage me and walk with me.

My supports are plentiful. There are those in my extended family who have been incredible in their understanding and support. I have had, and continue to have, friends and neighbours that were there for me when I needed them. It's interesting to see how my mental health improves with a phone call, a coffee date, a social outing, or a round of golf with friends.

In my commitment to staying mindful of my mental health, it's crucial for me to regularly consult with a mental health professional if I notice any decline in my well-being. Similar to many aspects of life, upkeep is essential. It's tempting to overlook warning signs and settle into complacency when things feel amiss. During such times, I actively seek assistance. It's fascinating to observe how my thought patterns shift when a professional acknowledges and validates my experiences, while also empowering me to utilize effective tools for cultivating a healthier self.

The Journey Continues

One morning recently, as I drank my coffee and caught up with news, I read an article forewarning of wacky weather in the coming winter. It suggested we would probably have some cold periods, maybe even a few outbreaks of bitter cold at some points, but also some milder periods as well. I chuckled at that because, quite frankly, that sounds like a normal winter and not wacky at all.

That is the analogy I like to use with my mental health. There are times, whether for an hour or a day, anxiety pays a visit, or my mood is subdued. But I know that like the weather in Manitoba it won't last. I also know that these ups and downs will happen in the future.

It becomes a matter of managing my mental health. Through awareness, acceptance, and an effort to be more intentional, I can weather those fluctuations. Utilizing and sticking with the things that help when I do experience a bad spell, I can rest assured it isn't forever. That gives me the ability to experience life as best possible.

In the introduction of this book, I told you about referring to myself as the Recovering Farmer. To remind you, recovering means to return to a former state of well being, prosperity and emotional balance. Years ago, when I first became familiar with the term recovering alcoholic, I sometimes wondered why it was recovering and not recovered. Today that term makes so much sense. Recovering is a process that takes time and, in some cases, can take the rest of your life.

By now you are well aware of my mental health. Clearly that's a journey that continues. Physically I am doing as well as can be expected, at least for today. Notice my paranoia; I often think I

Chapter 16 What Works for Me: Taming the Beast

have one foot in the grave. As I suggested in an earlier chapter, I hate going to the doctor because sure as the sun coming up in the east, the doctor will find some incurable disease. I certainly would not attempt to run a marathon. But that's fine. I was never able to do so and not sure I would want to.

I blew our retirement in the 90s. At the time, I enjoyed that. Today I think differently. As it turns out, my wife says I need to work till noon the day of my funeral. And, as someone suggested, I will probably be half an hour late because I will need to finish up some paperwork. That's not all bad as I know that just sitting around would not help my mental health. So as long as I am capable, I will keep working. A bonus is that I really enjoy the work I do.

But there is more to prosperity than just the financial aspect. I am reminded every single day that my wealth extends far beyond what I could have ever hoped for. I am blessed with the mental capacity and opportunity to make a living. Beyond that, I have the privilege of sharing my life with a truly wonderful family. I am able to savour the countless simple joys and experiences that life has to offer. From the warmth of a sunrise to the laughter of my loved ones, I find richness in every facet of my existence.

Over the years, as I have talked about recovering, I often allude to the fact that the equanimity piece in recovery has been challenging for me. Just to remind us, equanimity means having mental and emotional stability especially in difficult or challenging situations. I seem to always be under stress, whether real or perceived, which leaves me feeling anxious. And I often suggest that my anxiety manifests itself in road rage. Perhaps calling it road rage is overstating it a tad. Each time I head out on the highway, I tell myself to be a good person. Then someone pulls out in front of me going less than the speed limit and then I have to wait till the next day to try again.

I am convinced that people forgot how to drive during the pandemic. Some time ago, due to circumstances, I needed to drive my wife to work. No problem. Just a thirty-minute drive on some of the busiest roads around Winnipeg during rush hour. The ultimate test.

What is up with people following me mere inches from my bumper? Slam on the brakes to no avail. Slow down so they can pass. They slow down but stay right there. Blood pressure is rising. Hear a comment from the passenger side about my speed. Look down, don't see an issue. Why are there two semis driving side by side below the freaking speed limit? Come on, let me pass already. And then there's another driver right on my butt again thinking he needs to get where he is going before me. But I can't move because of the semis. Give me a break. I seem to have this attitude that when you drive faster than 110 kilometers per hour, you're an idiot and when you drive slower than 110, you're an idiot. And maybe, just maybe, I am the idiot.

Then I was reminded of what someone once told me. They suggested that driving was like dancing on a crowded dance floor. You move with the flow. Sometimes you move in front of others, and at times you let others by. But keep listening to the music and enjoy the dance.

Well, let me tell you. As a young Mennonite it was a sin to dance. As I got older, I needed liquid courage to dance and found out quickly that I have two left feet. And after taking some dance lessons there seemed to be mutual agreement in this household that, perhaps, dancing wasn't necessary. Or was that only me thinking that? Whatever the case, trying to improve my thoughts about other drivers by comparing it to dancing was not working.

As I ventured home it hit me. I was particularly impatient, seemingly in a rush to get home. A rush to get back to my office, to do what? So I changed my thinking. I looked at my travels as an opportunity to face another day of virtual everything by taking a

Chapter 16   What Works for Me: Taming the Beast

deep breath, cranking up the radio, and enjoying the solitude of my ride. It was rather interesting how quickly the antics of other drivers just simply didn't matter.

Takeaway

In Chapter 1 I talked about the importance of naming the beast. As much as that is important, we also need to find ways of taming that beast. For some it's simple enough to get rid of that beast entirely. For others not so much. And if that is the case, we need to learn ways of taming it.

First and foremost, by naming the beast, we acknowledge that it is within us. If we don't acknowledge and accept that inner beast, we run the risk of our mental wellness suffering even more. By acknowledging and accepting it, we can also take steps in taming it.

There are countless ways that folks have found to do just that. I have mentioned many of the tools and tricks I use. But I also know there are others. There is no shortage of ideas when you spend any time on social media. I will at times scroll through reels on Instagram, and invariably I will come across another way of lessening my anxiety. I will learn new tricks to help me move beyond my depression. Some of them work, others don't. It's trial and error at best.

Always remember, you are not alone. When I started speaking publicly, I had many folks approach me and also open up about the journeys they were on. Through those conversations, I found out how others deal with stress, anxiety, and depression. We shared ideas and that added to my arsenal.

Be gentle with yourself. There will be days when it seems that nothing works. Don't give in to those dark thoughts when they seem to be in attack mode. Learn to talk back at them. Choosing to fight that beast when it rears its ugly head, is choosing to take a step forward. Be positive. If not today, tomorrow will be better.

Be proactive. Don't shy away from seeking professional help. Sometimes that is needed and helps in finding ways to deal with the beast inside.

I have been asked on numerous occasions why I avoid medication. That's a fair question. Many folks I talk to use medication and have great success. Let me be very clear on something here. I am not saying medication is not helpful. As I have said previously, I was on medication for a number of years. In retrospect, I am not convinced that they were of particular help during that time. Along with that I seemed to be experiencing many of the side effects that I was warned about. Having said that, I also understand that medications have improved greatly over the years and often don't have the side effects that I experienced.

I know from conversations with others that many individuals have learned what works for them. What works for others might be different from what works for you. It's a matter of awareness and discovery. Through consultations with professionals, in one-on-one conversations with others, or your independent research, choose the ways that will work for you. The beast may be inside you, but it can be tamed. Make life changes before life changes.

CHAPTER 17
A Random Act of Kindness: The Cuddle Hormone

It's late at night and I am up to my eyeballs in hog manure. The temperature is dropping fast, and the wind chill is making it virtually impossible to work without gloves. Because of the cold, everything is freezing up and not working right. Equipment is breaking down, and here I am, spending more hours alone trying to get things to work. Another evening where I missed supper with the family. Another day working in isolation. It feels like an eternity since I last had a conversation with someone other than myself. The lack of human connection is getting to me.

Farming can be a lonely occupation, whether we are working alone in a barn or spending countless hours alone on a tractor. The isolation can be devastating, and we know that isolation breeds illness. It contributes to an overwhelming stress that we often experience.

Over the previous chapters I have talked lots about recognizing and dealing with stress. To remind us, stress is a normal part of life. Long term stress can have a debilitating impact on us, both physically and emotionally. It can lead to mental illness. In the last chapter I outlined what has worked for me. I have suggested that what works for me may or may not work for others. However, there is one tool we all can use, have easy access to, and is relatively simple to use.

Human connection is important and works for stress release. The connection with self, with family, friends, and community, the importance of talking to others, the importance of helping others, and the importance of relationships all contribute to a decrease in stress and an increase in our mental wellbeing.

I experienced the positive effects of connection through a random act of kindness. Perhaps I need to restate that. I had obviously experienced it in the past but never recognized it for what it was.

While my mother was still alive, each of us as siblings would take charge of the annual Christmas get-together. This particular Christmas it was my sister's turn. That meant she planned the food, a program and, of course, any type of gift-giving.

I have to tell you that having grown up in a Mennonite home a program was always integral to a successful gathering. That program would consist of singing carols, reciting poems, and reading the Christmas story directly from the Bible. So whether one could sing or not, we all lent our voices to hearty renditions of every carol ever written. After that—and don't forget we had already spent well over an hour in church that morning—we could open presents. Sounds torturous, right? I suspect it probably was not as bad as it sounds.

Now, what I really wanted to share was an idea that my sister put forward that could be done instead of gifts. In her words, she suggested that "in lieu of a gift exchange we ask that each individual initiate and/or perform a specific and random charitable act of kindness and share those experiences with the rest of the family." What a novel idea. So let me tell you the story of my random act of kindness.

Chapter 17   A Random Act of Kindness: The Cuddle Hormone

Happens that my wife and I were in Sobeys picking up some groceries after an afternoon of meeting some family in Brandon. The line-ups were long and patience was running thin. As the customer in front of us was having her groceries rung up, I suggested to my wife that we offer to pay for them as our act of random kindness. Trust me. I had already done a mental calculation on her groceries and knew it would not break the bank.

My wife insisted that it was my family, hence I should take the lead in starting the conversation. She graciously moved aside, allowing me to proceed first and extend the offer. Initially, I stepped forward with resolve, but doubt crept in. I feared it might cause a scene, lead to embarrassment, or result in her viewing me as being weird. Despite these concerns, courage prevailed, and I went ahead with the offer.

Well, to be sure, the reaction was interesting. The cashier started laughing, a somewhat nervous laugh, and the customer gave me a questioning look. I assured them both that I was quite serious. The woman was flustered and wanted to know why. I suggested that we wanted to do this for her and wished her a Merry Christmas. She made the comment that it was good to see that there were still nice people around. And as she left, she wished us a Merry Christmas as well.

As we travelled home after that, I commented to my wife how good I felt. Yes, I had fulfilled my duties of doing a random act of kindness, but there was more to the sense of warmth I felt. I suggested that should I win a lottery I would go from store to store and randomly pay for people's groceries. In the moment, that connection I felt was more than any medication or drug could ever do. It was interesting how long that feeling stayed with me. It helped in removing that dark cloud that had been hanging over my head for far too long. And for some strange reason, I think I rediscovered what Christmas was meant to be.

There is an irony in all of this. I had written the above as a blog post. A day or so after having posted the blog, I mentioned it to a colleague. She told me that someone had told her the story because it had been in the Brandon Sun. I didn't say much, just thinking she had misspoken. Then someone else told me that there had been a letter to the editor about a similar story. I checked it out and was surprised to see that the lady whose groceries I had paid for had written the letter. The following is her letter.

> *A quick trip to the grocery store late in the afternoon on Saturday, Dec. 4 turned into quite a heartwarming experience for me. I was at Sobeys and was just about to pay for my groceries, when the man who was in line behind me said to the cashier "add that to mine, please."*
>
> *Shocked, I turned around and looked at the man with a puzzled look on my face. The cashier and I looked at each other, and then we both looked at the fellow who had just offered to pay for my groceries. I immediately said to him "What? Why would you want to do that? We don't even know each other." Which was true, we were complete strangers.*
>
> *The man then said to me, with a friendly smile, "I want to, I insist. Merry Christmas!" All I could say was, "Are you serious?" And he said, "Sure I am!" Of course, I politely declined his offer, and told him that it was very kind of him, but not necessary. He wouldn't take no for an answer. He seemed so genuine and sincere and kind, it brought tears to my eyes.*

Chapter 17   A Random Act of Kindness: The Cuddle Hormone

I told him, "There really are some wonderful people in this world." I thanked him from the bottom of my heart and wished him a very Merry Christmas.

I left the store with a big smile, tears in my eyes, and a warm heart. As soon as I got into my vehicle, I phoned my husband to tell him what had just happened to me! It was an incredibly kind gesture for one stranger to do for another.

After I left the store, I felt guilty. I thought to myself, maybe I should have stuck around to speak to him a little longer, I wish I would have asked him his name. I circled the parking lot, hoping to see him again, but didn't. I don't know why he chose me to be the recipient of his generosity, but it has affected me greatly. I appreciate what he did, although I wish that he would have chosen someone who needed it more than me.

That is why I have decided that I must pay it forward ... and I will. I hope that the man who was in line behind me at Sobeys on Saturday reads this. I haven't stopped thinking about him, or what he did, or why he even did it for that matter. I want to apologize for not asking him his name or waiting for him so we could speak to one another a little longer.

I do want to thank him yet again, and I want him to know how wonderful I think he is, and how his kindness has affected me. I would also like to once again wish him a very Merry Christmas! Without knowing it, a complete stranger has made this

Christmas one that I will never forget. Think about how we could all be that person in someone else's Christmas memories.

That rather innocent act on my part had provided something positive for two people. The lady I bought the groceries for and I, went home that night having made a connection that resonated with both of us and gave us both a more positive outlook on life.

The Buddha said, "If you knew, as I do, the power of giving, you would not let a single meal pass without sharing some of it." He taught that when we truly understand the power of generosity, we experience how it brings joy to the giver as well as to the receiver.

Takeaway

We have all heard of the different chemicals or hormones we have in our brain. A lot of the discussion around my mental illness has been about Serotonin and Dopamine. But there is another one not as often discussed. I am talking about Oxytocin, often known as the cuddle hormone. It is also known as a trust hormone and love hormone.

Oxytocin serves as a vital factor in reducing stress and regulating blood pressure. It promotes the desire for physical contact, communication, empathy, compassion, and care. Additionally, it contributes to fostering optimism, elevating self-esteem, and nurturing trust. This hormone is released during a range of interpersonal interactions, including hugging, handshakes, thoughts about others, or even mere eye contact across a room.

Adding kindness, a quality of being friendly and considerate, to the mix just adds to our mental wellbeing. Kindness is a behaviour so all of us have it in us and can use it. It comes with significant positive health benefits. It produces serotonin in our brains, so can serve as a natural antidepressant. And both the receiver and giver, in an act of kindness, will feel an increase in oxytocin.

Chapter 17 A Random Act of Kindness: The Cuddle Hormone

It has been said that we are the loneliest society in history. We see and hear about increasing cases of anxiety and depression. There are reports of increased suicides and accidental overdoses. It seems rather ironic that we have all the technology available to connect with others, but the truth of the matter is that we are not connecting in the true sense of the word. Interaction with others, which produces joy and fulfillment, is more lacking than ever.

Connection fulfills one of our most fundamental human needs. It involves the sharing of experiences, the expression of relatable feelings, and the exchange of similar ideas. The prevalence of stress in our lives often damages our ability to connect with others as we tend to isolate ourselves and conceal our struggles.

However, when we invest in building relationships, open up to one another, engage in meaningful conversations, and extend acts of kindness, we liberate ourselves from the constraints of our self-imposed limitations. This freedom allows us to think beyond conventional boundaries, revealing a world that we knew could exist but couldn't see from within the confines of our self-imposed box we put ourselves in. Through this process, we unearth new directions, redefine our identity, and discover a renewed sense of purpose. And you may find that the one giving receives the most.

Chapter 18
Working on a Puzzle: Don't You Quit

It has been another day of cycling, spending time at the beach and all other things that come with camping. As the sun sets, I sit by the fire, chatting with my kids and their partners. The laughter of my grandchildren fills the air. As the moon rises and the stars come out, a peculiar sensation I have longed for slowly takes hold within me. Without any warning, I spontaneously say the words that have been welling up within me: "I can't believe how happy I feel." My kids are rather surprised, not quite sure whether they have heard right. They try to reconcile those words with moments that have often been veiled by life's challenges. Gradually the surprise gives way to smiles, and in that moment, a glimmer of hope ignites within us all. It has been a while since this warmth filled our hearts, but now, as the fire crackles and the night unfolds, there is a sense of promise in the possibility of brighter days ahead.

I suspect most of us, at some point in our life, have reflected on the type of picture our life is forming. As I have alluded to, I often viewed my life as a waste. I became disillusioned. Even trying to imagine some kind of picture was difficult. For all intents

Chapter 18 Working on a Puzzle: Don't You Quit

and purposes, it appeared I had thrown paint against the wall and was hoping for a picture. With each life event, career choice, or relationships, it was like flinging another gallon of paint at the wall. There was a lack of clarity. In fact, I would suggest there was no picture at all. It seemed to be an unmitigated mess.

I often wondered if things were meant to be. I have made mention of looking back and not liking the view. I questioned it when a colleague suggested that had I not experienced what I had, I couldn't do what I am doing today. In the introduction I stated that writing about my journey had been therapeutic. I came to a better understanding that, in spite of my mental illness, there had been many positives in my life. As I mapped out my journey a picture did begin to emerge.

I saw how each step in the journey was inextricably linked to the last, culminating in where I am today. I came to understand that the journey continues and that each day or week or month is filled with more discovery. I learned that who I was in the past does not dictate who I am today. I found out that I need to reassess on a continuous basis to ensure that I keep moving forward and not get bogged down by slipping into the ruts of the past. I learned that life is full of uncertainties, unknowns, and can, at times, feel like a mystery.

In extending the analogy of trying to form a picture of my life, I go back to what I wrote in Chapter 11. I talked about life being like a puzzle and how, at times, we feel uncomfortable with certain pieces and where they belong. I have come to the understanding that my life is, indeed, a puzzle, and each step in the journey represents another piece I can incorporate. Many aspects that previously seemed perplexing or out of place now find their context. A coherent picture is emerging. Allow me to elaborate.

A typical puzzle, particularly the ones my wife enjoys, has four corners. These corners serve as the foundation for the entire puzzle and begin to take shape early in life. Upon contemplation of my own life, I identify the four corners as family, friends, career, and health. These corners act as the borders that outline the picture that is yet to unfold.

Although there were times I would have preferred to take some pieces out, I know they are important in the big picture. Each piece contributes to the whole. Clearly there are aspects of the picture that don't look so good. When I step back to see what the picture is looking like, I see areas where I made mistakes, made poor decisions, and don't particularly care for what I see. But no matter how many flaws there may be, seeing those help me in doing better in the future. It helps in ensuring the best outcome possible.

I am a husband to a wife who has stuck with me through all my challenges. Even when her marriage involved me becoming someone she sometimes wished she had never been married to, she helped me become a more preferable husband. A wife that has supported me as I faced the challenges of mental illness. A wife that encouraged me to write this book, and when I became discouraged, was there to give me the push I needed. I know there were times when she would have liked to have changed some of the pieces I was putting in my puzzle. Surely that corner of the puzzle could easily have come apart without her support and guidance. And who knows what it might have looked like if that had happened?

One of the coolest things I have ever been called is "Dad." I am a father to three amazing kids who supported as best possible when things were looking bleak. Kids who were able to put aside the anguish of seeing their father spiral out of control and show a love that helped me become a better father. And those kids have found partners who have stood with them when their father was not well. They have also been an incredible encouragement for me. In my mind, an indication of success is when your kids, as adults, want to spend time with you. That makes me a success.

Chapter 18 Working on a Puzzle: Don't You Quit

Even cooler than being called Dad is being called "Grandpa." I am a grandpa to amazing grandkids. Kids who show an unconditional love. Kids who encourage me to see beyond the anxieties and concerns of today. Kids who make me want to be better and stay better.

Now that I have a clearer understanding of my own puzzle, I recognize how others, especially my wife, kids, their partners, and my grandkids, play a crucial role in helping me assemble the pieces. I am aware that there are moments when I fall short of being the person I aspire to be, temporarily disrupting the arrangement of pieces. However, my family understands this and supports me through those times. Thanks to these relationships, we journey together, each working on our individual puzzles. Together, we witness the gradual formation of each others' unique pictures.

I have friends whom I have been able to talk to over the years. Friends who have been there, have checked on me, and have supported me as I struggled to find my way. Friends that listened without judgement, that challenged me when I needed the extra push, friends that encouraged me to take a step forward when that seemed too overwhelming for me. Without those friends the puzzle would be missing a significant part of the picture.

For some time, I had wondered about the path I had taken with what now feels like multiple careers. I have mentioned regrets that I went farming. I questioned my abilities for being a mediator. I downplayed my passion for mental health. With my approach, each time there was a change, I would take apart that part of the puzzle. But I have learned that I need to keep all those pieces intact. The changing path of my career doesn't change the pieces. I was of the opinion that being a farmer or being involved in agricultural politics or being a mediator or being a counsellor meant I had to remove pieces each time my work changed or other opportunities came. I now see how the pieces all fit together.

Clearly my health, particularly my mental health, has played a significant role in my life. When that corner of the puzzle first began things were a real mess. But over time, and with significant effort, that has taken shape as well. When I look at some of those pieces, I don't like what I see. But I also understand that the past does not dictate what the future may bring. I also get that being reminded of the past helps me in ensuring a better tomorrow. The pieces are making sense and are fitting together as they should.

Through awareness, acceptance, and an effort to be more intentional I can keep working at the puzzle. Utilizing and sticking with the things that help when I do experience a bad spell, I can rest assured it isn't forever. I know I am no longer who I was but also know I am not yet who I will become. That gives me the ability to experience life as best possible. That lets me be who I am, because if I am not who I am, then who am I?

My puzzle is not complete. The work continues. But with the clarity I have found, working on this puzzle called life has become more enjoyable. There is a certain mystery of what other pieces will show up and how they will fit, knowing full well that they may not always be pieces I like. But that's okay. After all, my life, my journey, is one of discovery.

Takeaway

As I reflect on my journey and the puzzle of life I've been assembling, I can't help but recall the words of John Greenleaf Whittier, a poet who faced significant mental illness in his own life. He was an advocate for the abolition of slavery in the mid-1800s, and his perseverance in the face of adversity has always been an inspiration to me. The first and last verse of one of his poems, which I've committed to memory and often recite, seems to resonate with the very essence of the puzzle I've been describing. It's a timeless

Chapter 18 Working on a Puzzle: Don't You Quit

reminder that we should never give up, even when life's challenges seem insurmountable.

His poem "Don't Quit" encapsulates the very spirit of my journey, and I hope it can inspire you as it has inspired me. The following two verses have guided me through my struggles, reminding me that even when life's puzzle pieces don't fit perfectly, I must persevere. Our journeys, like our puzzles, are full of uncertainty, but it's in these moments of uncertainty that we truly discover ourselves.

Don't Quit

When things go wrong, as they sometimes will,
When the road you're trudging seems all uphill,
When the funds are low and the debts are high,
And you want to smile, but you have to sigh,
When care is pressing you down a bit,
Rest if you must, but don't you quit.

Success is failure turned inside out
The silver tint in the clouds of doubt,
And you never can tell how close you are,
It might be near when it seems afar.
So stick to the fight when you're hardest hit.
It's when things seem worst you must not quit.

John Greenleaf Whittier

Acknowledgements

Writing a book entails a certain skillset. It requires an ability to utilize one's imagination. Even when writing about real life events, there is a need to be able to tell a story with enough detail to vividly portray a picture. The narratives must flow seamlessly to engage the reader and prevent them from getting lost. Moreover, it must be written in a manner that captivates the reader's interest from start to finish.

That skillset did not come easy for me. In 2010 I was challenged to write a regular blog post. Known for rarely turning down challenges, I dove right in. The planning was minimal, and I had no end of ideas and thoughts that I could write about. I also recognized my limitations. I soon discovered that my train of thought, if it didn't leave the station without me, allowed for about six hundred words before reaching the next stop.

Adding further to the challenge was that I am not a prolific typer. I did take a typing course in grade ten. One day, towards the end of the school year, the teacher was looking over my shoulder and noticed that I was typing using only two fingers. He told me I needed to start over, never checked back, and gave me a passing grade. Since then, I've been doing all my writings with just two fingers. So you can well imagine how those two fingers have a difficult time keeping up to my brain. Then again, not convinced that ten fingers could.

Furthermore, I wasn't sure what I would write about. It had been suggested to me by some that stories from my farming days could be captivating. Others thought my encounters with mental health and addiction would make for a compelling read. I wasn't convinced that any of that would produce enough material for a book. All of that left me wondering how I could write a book.

But without giving too much thought to any of the above, I started. As I penned my thoughts, I found myself unsure if I was writing a memoir, a self-help book, or a collection of stories. It was only when someone suggested it could be all of the above that I felt a renewed sense of purpose. I finally completed something that had been in the works for many years. With the unwavering support and encouragement from friends, family, and mentors, I discovered the wherewithal to push beyond my perceived boundaries. The process, though arduous, became a testament to the power of community and belief, making the seemingly impossible, possible.

My wife Rose was a staunch and supportive partner in this project. First and foremost, she has walked the journey with me. She encouraged me when I felt like giving up, both in life and in writing this book. She took the time to read my manuscript and provided input. And then I asked her to read it again, and she did. In addition, she remained patient during those times I was hunkered down in my office working on this book and not doing everything else a husband should be doing.

My kids, Cody, Tony and Roxy, were there in my darkest times. They showed me love when it would have been easier to walk away. Together with Jocelyn and Luke, when they joined our family, they supported each other, they supported me, and they walked with me. They read my manuscript, they suggested changes, but most of all they cheered me on.

My grandkids, Kai, Kenna, Liv, Dash, Harper and Rylan, and any that might be added in the future, created wonderful distractions

Acknowledgements

when I needed them most. As I said in the book, being called grandpa is the coolest thing ever. I just want them to know that someday when they read this book, them being them encouraged me to continue writing.

Tony, thank you for the deep dive into the stuff I had written. You took the time to let me know when I had stepped outside the lines, when certain content did nothing for the betterment of the book and when my language was not appropriate for the times. I can only imagine how often you must have felt exasperated with what I had written. And I would be remiss in not thanking you and Jocelyn for the cover design. Not something I had envisioned, but it grew on me quickly.

Dr. Cory has profoundly impacted my life, and I will always be indebted to her. She meticulously connected dots for me, showing me a pathway I never thought existed. With her unwavering support, she encouraged me to navigate through challenges, guided me with wisdom, and provided invaluable help every step of the way. Thanks to her, I have the confidence to pursue a future filled with promise and possibilities.

My neighbor Michael, an accomplished author, graciously shared his wealth of expertise with me. He dedicated his time to thoroughly read my work, offering insightful critiques and constructive ideas. His encouragement was a beacon of support in my creative journey, guiding me through the intricacies of storytelling. I am acutely aware of the debt of gratitude I owe him for his invaluable mentorship and unwavering support.

Kim, Bri, Deb, and Miranda, I am sincerely grateful for your invaluable insights and suggestions regarding my initial manuscript. Your contributions, though I can't be certain if you read every word, have undeniably enhanced the book's quality. Your encouragement fueled my determination to refine my work.

To all those that have walked with me on my journey, I say thanks. In retrospect I find it interesting how someone would always be there when I needed it most. You took the time to walk with me, listen without judgement and encouraged me when I needed it most. Without you this story would have turned out much differently, if written at all.

I extend my heartfelt gratitude to the dedicated team at Friesen Press for their invaluable assistance. Their expertise in translating my writings from Mennonite to English was truly commendable. Despite my occasional impatience and frustration, they remained steadfastly patient and understanding, guiding me through the intricacies of the publishing process with kindness and support.

In conclusion, I want to express my sincere thanks to you, the reader. Your decision to read my book, whether out of curiosity or genuine interest, is deeply appreciated. Even if you perceive my words as primarily for my own benefit, know that writing them was a source of encouragement for me. If any part of my writing resonates with you, I sincerely hope that it serves as a catalyst for inspiration in your own journey. May the connection forged through these words offer solace and encouragement as you navigate your path forward.

About the Author

Gerry Friesen, AKA The Recovering Farmer, grew up on a farm near Wawanesa, Manitoba. In 1983 he took over the family farm and operated it till 2007 when other interests demanded more and more of his time.

From 1990 to 2005, Gerry was heavily involved in agricultural "politics" serving on the boards of Manitoba Pork Est., Manitoba Pork Marketing Co-op, the Canadian Pork Council, and Keystone Agricultural Producers.

In 2000, he was appointed to the Manitoba Farm Mediation Board and in 2007 began working with the Manitoba Farm and Rural Stress Line. In 2021 he was a co-founder of the Manitoba Farmer Wellness Program and now serves as the program's Chief Administrative Officer.

Gerry's passion is in helping others find solutions for the various issues that life throws at us. A combination of his own journey with anxiety and depression, training in conflict resolution and intensive counseling training, provide him the tools to help others who are struggling.

Through his company, Signature Mediation, he provides conflict management services to various organizations. In addition, he enjoys presenting and facilitating workshops on mental wellbeing.

Gerry is a recipient of the 2010 Manitoba Pork Council Friend of the Industry Award in recognition of "providing emotional support and expertise to help farmers cope with financial and emotional stress in their darkest days."

In 2019 his interview, on the Impact Farming Show titled A Farmer's Journey Through Stress, Depression and Anxiety, was the winner in the Best of CAMA (Canadian Agri-Marketing Association) Podcast category.

And in 2020 he was the runner up for the Canadian Federation of Agriculture Bridgit Rivoire Champions of Agricultural Mental Health award, recognizing his passion and advocacy for mental wellness in the farming community.

Gerry and his wife live in La Salle, Manitoba. They are parents to three kids and are now enjoying life with six grandkids.

Printed in Canada